© Bradley K. Ross

About the Author

HILLARY CARLIP, author of *Girl Power*, has written commentaries for NPR, and is a performer and artist. She is the creator of the acclaimed personal essay Web site freshyarn.com, and she lives in Los Angeles. You can find out more about Hillary at her Web site, hillarycarlip.com.

Queen of the Oddballs

Queen of the Oddballs

And Other True Stories from a Life Unaccording to Plan

Hillary Carlip

Harper

An Imprint of HarperCollinsPublishers

Some of the names and identifying characteristics have been changed. Although these are all true stories, some of the dialogue has been re-created, based on my memory of the incidents.

Grateful acknowledgment to Sherry Rayn Barnett for the photographs of Carly Simon on page 44, Carole King on page 67, and Nina Simone on page 206; Vaughan Cruickshank, Tasmania, for the photograph of the scooters on page 239; Claudia Kunin for the photograph of Angel and the Reruns on page 155; and huge thanks to Carly Simon for graciously allowing me to reprint her letter.

FIRST EDITION

Embroidered illustrations by Jenny Hart

Library of Congress Cataloging-in-Publication Data
    Carlip, Hillary.
        Queen of the oddballs : and other true stories from a life unaccording to plan / by Hillary Carlip.
            p. cm.
        ISBN-10: 0-06-087883-5
        ISBN-13: 978-0-06-087883-2
        1. Carlip, Hillary. 2. Entertainers—United States—Biography. I. Title.
    PN2287.C269A3 2006
    791.092—dc22   2005056700

06 07 08 09 10 ID/RRD 10 9 8 7 6 5 4 3 2 1

For Mom, Dad, and Bro, who made me everything I am today.
And for Mackie, who loves everything I am today.

Contents

Contents

Queen of the Oddballs

1965

✳ "The Name Game," sung by Shirley Ellis, hits # 3 on the charts. Everyone sings their own name in the song but I sing "Chuck." "Chuck Chuck Bo Buck Bonana-Fana Fo Fuck!!" Tee hee. (All right, I'm only eight years old.)

✳ Months after Malcolm X is assassinated and Martin Luther King Jr. leads a march from Selma to Montgomery, Alabama, demanding voting rights for blacks, the Watts Riots erupt during a routine traffic stop. The rioting lasts for six days and requires 14,000 National Guardsmen to be called. I watch on our black-and-white television to make sure my black friend, Pat Wallace, is not one of the 4,000 people arrested or thirty-four killed.

✳ A babysitter takes my brother and me to the Hollywood Bowl to see the Beatles LIVE IN CONCERT! I wear a fab Carnaby Street outfit—short print miniskirt with matching tie and cap, and purple windowpane stockings—and scream with all the other screaming fans throughout the entire concert.

* See Miss Jane Hathaway from *The Beverly Hillbillies* buying meatballs at the Bel Air Market down the street from our house.

* Just a few months before they score their first #1 hit song in America, "(I Can't Get No) Satisfaction," the Rolling Stones are arrested in London for public urination. Every time I hear Bob Dylan's new song, "Like a Rolling Stone," I get the urge to pee.

* Go see my fave new movie, *What's New Pussycat?*, two less times than my mother sees her fave new movie, *The Sound of Music* (me, four; Mom, six).

* *A Charlie Brown Christmas* is broadcast on TV for the first time. I ask my parents when they'll air *A Charlie Brown Chanukah*.

* The Beatles perform on the *Ed Sullivan Show*. I try to photograph them, but when the pics are developed, all you can see is a big glare where the TV set was, and my brother's feet in the frame.

Hilly Golightly

What do you do when you feel so invisible you can't sleep without a light on, afraid that in the dark you just might vanish entirely? Simple. Become someone interesting enough to be noticed. And that's exactly what I did when I was eight years old.

I took on different personas the way other kids tried on clothes. I Frugged and Mashed Potatoed incessantly for an entire month when I was being a go-go dancer from *Hullabaloo!* After that, for several weeks I yanked my short hair into pigtails, wore all black, and skulked around the house and school, acting "creepy, kooky, mysterious, and spooky," when I was being Wednesday from *The Addams Family.* A few months later, hooked on Gerry and the Pacemakers, I sang and spoke only in an English accent. How much more interesting could I get?

The answer came one night when my parents were out and my ten-year-old brother, our teenage babysitter, and I watched the movie *Breakfast at Tiffany's* on TV. I was smitten with Holly Golightly. Daring and darling, she shoplifted and had only one friend, her cat named Cat. She was strong and independent, saying things like "You don't have to worry. I've taken care of myself for a long time." Those words rang so true to me.

My parents, Mim and Bob, both on the short side, each with open, reassuring expressions and sympathetic smiles, took on full-time jobs as compassionate listeners to everyone else's problems—the gardener's, the grocery checkout clerk's, the mailman's. In fact on more than one occasion, they invited our mailman, Felix, to join us for dinner at the end of his route. They helped the neighbor's daughter get into private school, found a job for the pharmacist's son, and took in Esperanza, a teenage boarder from Guatemala. Whatever remained of my parents' energy was sucked up by my hyperactive, rebellious older brother, Howard, whose constant demands for attention began as early as when, at six months old, he literally threw himself out of his crib.

I was definitely noticed when I started acting like Holly Golightly. Unfortunately, it wasn't quite the sort of attention I had desired.

*   *   *

I sat on a hard wooden chair in the principal's office, my arms hidden behind my back, when my parents walked in.

Mr. Shelton, the principal at Bellagio Road Elementary School, sported a head of bushy gray hair and matching moustache, making him look like Larry Tate from *Bewitched*. I wished I could twitch my nose like Samantha Stephens and turn myself into something tiny and unnoticeable, like a postage stamp.

"Your daughter's being suspended from school," he told my parents.

"From the third grade? Why?" My mother was stunned.

"What did she do?" my dad asked.

"Her teacher, Mrs. Renzoli, caught her on the playground smoking cigarettes."

"What?" My mother shrieked as my dad's eyes darted around, searching for an ashtray to stub out his Benson and Hedges.

"Hill, why were you smoking?" Mom asked.

I shrugged. My dad excused himself, opened the office door, stomped out his cigarette on the sidewalk right outside, then hurried back in. "Answer your mother," he said.

I slowly pulled my arms from behind my back, revealing my mom's black, elbow-length gloves that, on me, went up to my shoulders. "I was being Holly Golightly."

"Who?" Mr. Shelton asked. It figured he didn't know who she was.

"She's a character from *Breakfast at Tiffany's*," my mother responded. "Hillary saw the movie recently, and I guess it made an impression."

"I tried to get a long cigarette holder, but I couldn't find one anywhere," I said, confident in that moment that my parents were now on my side, having to explain to the ignorant principal who Holly Golightly was.

But they weren't at all on my side. In fact, my latest shenanigans not only got me suspended, they also resulted in my being sent to Dr. Eleanor Troupe, Child Psychologist.

*　　*　　*

"Please, Mom, don't make me go," I begged at the door of Dr. Troupe's office, a fading salmon pink one-story duplex dwarfed into near oblivion by the high-rises on busy Wilshire Boulevard in Westwood Village. "I'll do anything you want if I don't have to go—name it."

My mother took a deep breath and exhaled any doubts she may have had. "Sorry, Hill. Your father and I have made our decision, and it's final."

We stepped into a waiting room, and I begrudgingly sat on the sofa—but it was difficult to maintain an attitude with my 3'10" body swallowed up by puffy pink pillows.

Dr. Troupe came out to greet us, and the sight made me gasp out loud: a woman older than my grandmother, her body was distorted in several directions at once. She limped in on her left leg, which was bent to the right, while her torso twisted in the opposite direction. Her right hand looked like a claw, raised in a permanent fist near her shoulder, and her mouth warped to the left, creating a bucktoothed, snarly smile.

"You must be Hillary," she sputtered. "I've heard a lot about you, and you sound like a very interesting young lady. I'm very happy to meet you."

Though I was terrified by her deformities, this was the first time anyone had called me interesting. That was enough for me to willingly follow her into her office. She motioned with her eyes—the only uncrossed thing on her body—for me to sit in a maroon leather chair. My mother called out from the waiting room, "I'll pick you up in an hour," then left.

Dr. Troupe pointed with her claw to a large glass jar filled to the top with a mix of Brach's chewy chocolate and caramel squares wrapped snugly in smooth plastic. "Help yourself," she said.

I did as she opened a cupboard and pulled out a board game. "You ever play Clue?"

"Sure. I played a lot recently when I was being the Girl from U.N.C.L.E. Well, not *the* Girl from U.N.C.L.E.—that part's already taken by Stefanie Powers, who plays her on TV."

"I see. Is she a detective?" Dr. Troupe asked as she opened the box and clumsily spilled out the miniature lead pipe, rope, revolver, and candlestick.

"Yep. For my birthday I got a Sixfinger spy kit." I told her all about the plastic, flesh-colored extra finger that shot cap bombs, SOS flares, and message missiles and had a hidden clicker so I could communicate in code with anyone who understood the secret language.

"Fascinating. So who do you click messages with?"

"Uh, no one I know understands the secret language. So, nobody."

Dr. Troupe chuckled and winked at me—at least it looked like she did.

"Well, then, who do you want to be?"

I felt my cheeks grow hot. I didn't know how to answer her question.

"I'll be Miss Scarlet," she announced.

Hillary Carlip

Phew. She meant in *the game*. Okay. "I'll be Colonel Mustard."

"Good choice." She smiled her twisted smile right at me and handed me the dark yellow game piece. As we played Clue, Dr. Troupe casually asked me all sorts of questions. "What do like doing most in school?" "Do you have any hobbies?" "What's your dog's name?" After I took a secret passage from the study, I announced that Mrs. Peacock had used the lead pipe in the conservatory, and I won the game. Dr. Troupe squealed in delight. Usually when I won at home Howard would sit on my chest, pin me down, and torture me by letting out a long line of drool, trying to suck up the saliva before it dripped into my face—sometimes succeeding, more often not. I liked Dr. Troupe.

Then she looked at her watch. "I want to ask you one more thing," she said. "Why do you think you're here?"

I shrugged. "My teacher, Mrs. Renzoli, turned me in. She doesn't like me much."

"Why would you say that?"

"She's always telling me to keep quiet, settle down." I paused, then added, "I guess I don't like her much, either. She has a pointy nose and wears a long black coat, so she looks like an old crow."

Dr. Troupe laughed heartily.

"Well, I guess it's really my parents' fault. They're the ones who made me come."

"You know they sent you here because they care about you, don't you?"

I wiped my bangs to the side of my forehead, as if making room for the thought to sink in.

"Well, our time is up today," Dr. Troupe said, "but we'll talk more about this next week. I look forward to seeing you Thursday."

To my surprise, I looked forward to seeing her, too.

I visited Dr. Troupe weekly. We chatted while we played Lie Detector, Sorry, Careers, and Operation, which was a bit challenging for her as she tried to remove the patient's "funny bone" with her clawed hand without setting off the buzzer. Her questions always turned out to be compliments. "Why do you think your parents wouldn't love a neat kid like you?" "Do you have a lot of friends? You must." "Why do you want to be other people when you're such a fascinating young lady yourself?"

One late afternoon, two months into our sessions, I was in the car on the way to my appointment when my mother announced that this would be my last visit.

"Why? Why can't I keep seeing Dr. Troupe?" I cried.

"She says you're fine."

"So? She's my friend." I wiped my nose on the sleeve of my Snoopy sweatshirt.

"We hired her to help you, and she said she's done all she can."

When my mother pulled up to the fading duplex, I stepped out of the car and slammed the door. My mom leaned over and rolled down the window. "Sorry, Hill."

I tried to be brave. I cried only once during the whole session, and it wasn't even when I lost a round of Parcheesi. The hour passed, and we said good-bye. Dr. Troupe bent over, even more than she already was, and she hugged me with her one good arm. She whispered in my ear, "Just try being yourself. I think you're gonna like what you see. I know I do."

For days after that last visit I refused to leave my bedroom. I was heartbroken over losing the only person who seemed interested in me. Besides, I planned to try and follow her advice to just be myself, but first I had to practice in private. Over the next few weeks, despite my urges, I didn't take on any new personas. One night at the dinner table, I excitedly told my parents the good news of the day. "Mrs. Renzoli made me Blind Monitor!"

"Ya mean you watch the blind kids in your class?" Howard teased.

"Very funny." I continued, "A bunch of times during the day I open and close the Venetian blinds. In the morning, before the class arrives, I open all the blinds that cover the windows on two walls. At rest time I close them, then reopen them fifteen minutes later, then close them again at the end of each day. If we see a film, I get to open and close them two more times and—"

"Okay, Hill. That's great," my father said.

"But I'm not done—"

"We get it. You're on another talkathon. Can't I have some quiet when I get home after a long day at work?"

My brother laughed. I lifted a glazed carrot coin from my plate and threw it at him. He scooped up a spoonful of mashed potatoes and flung them at me.

My father's bottom lip began to curl. "Both of you go to your rooms. NOW!"

"Fine," I snapped, throwing my napkin on the table. "I might as well be alone. Nobody listens to me anyway." I stormed past my mother, who sighed heavily.

Later, when everyone was in bed, I sneaked downstairs and turned on the little black-and-white TV in the den. The movie *Pollyanna* was on. Hayley Mills starred as the optimistic and inquisitive orphan who sneaks out of her second-story window to attend a carnival and falls out of a tree, seriously hurting her leg. The whole town rallies, sending flowers and showering her with attention.

The next morning I put on a short, plaid dress, went to school, and colored my knee with an Indian red crayon. All day long I limped dramatically, due to my "injury," and almost every classmate asked me what happened. "Fell out of a tree," I sighed bravely.

At 3:00, as I was lowering the blinds, Mrs. Renzoli crowed, "Hillary, stay after class, please."

I was scared she was going to send me to the principal's office again, but when I remembered my punishment last time—Dr. Eleanor Troupe—I actually got excited. Maybe I'd be able to see my misshapen friend once more and eat caramels and play games and talk as much as I wanted to.

"Just go to your seat, kid," Mrs. Renzoli said without looking up from her desk. She called everyone "kid." She sat grading spelling tests. I knew I had misspelled "ukulele," but I couldn't possibly be getting in trouble for that, could I? A few minutes later, my mother arrived. This was unusual, as I always rode the school bus home.

"So," she asked, "what's Hillary done now?"

Mrs. Renzoli stood up and rearranged her long black coat, aligning the buttons that had strayed to the side. "Don't worry, Mrs. Carlip. This time I have good news. Out of all the students here at Bellagio Road Elementary School, the faculty has chosen your daughter to appear on the CBS television show Art Linkletter's *House Party*."

"What?" I called out. "Me on TV?"

My mother beamed.

"Your daughter's quite a character," Mrs. Renzoli said.

*   *   *

As my television debut approached, I began to feel deliriously happy. Now for sure I'd be interesting and worthy of attention. Every afternoon I watched kids saying "the darndest things" on Art Linkletter's *House Party* and eagerly waited for my turn.

Finally, on a humid Thursday morning during summer vacation, my mother and brother dropped me off at an empty Bellagio Road Elementary School. I wished someone other than Mrs. Renzoli was around to witness the long, black stretch limousine parked in front, ready to whisk us off to CBS Studios, but my disappointment didn't last long. I leaped into the back, careful not to wrinkle the simple, sleeveless yellow-and-white striped shirt my parents had picked out at Bullocks department store for me to wear. I straightened the white Peter Pan collar and retied the bouncy bow that sat on my left hip. I felt carefree and sassy.

My mom called out, "We'll see you at the studio."

"Why can't you guys ride with us?" I asked.

As she stepped into the limo, Mrs. Renzoli answered, "Your teacher is the designated chaperone, kid. That's how they do it at CBS."

As we started to drive away, I noticed that along with her black coat Mrs. Renzoli was wearing beige orthopedic shoes that tied down the sides. She sucked on Clorets, which made her smell like peppermint and coated her tongue dark green. I was shaking with excitement as I pushed and pulled a button that made the tinted windows go up and down. Then I turned on a little television set. I switched the channels back and forth as Mrs. Renzoli poured a cocktail from a bar stocked with tall bottles and fluted glasses. She downed her drink then poured herself another, even though it was morning. She didn't say one word to me as we sped down Sunset Boulevard, past the brown August hills. She just kept drinking, and when we stopped at traffic signals, she'd lower the window and wave at strangers.

A half hour later, we pulled up to CBS Television City at Beverly and Fairfax, and a tall man in a suit with a lot of Brylcreem in his hair ushered us inside. As we walked down the shiny hallways, I kept my eyes peeled, hoping to spot Lucille Ball or one of the girls from *Petticoat Junction*. No such luck. But we did see Red Skelton rehearsing his show, and he shook my hand. I had never seen him in anything other than black-and-white. He was so . . . well, *red*.

The Brylcreem man whisked me into a tiny room, where the three other kids who would appear on the show with me were waiting. The one other girl wore a fancy lace dress and shiny patent leather shoes; the two boys wore dark suits and ties. I was embarrassed. They were all dressed for a formal party, while I was dressed for a hootenanny.

A brunette woman who looked like a movie star sauntered in and introduced herself as Dorothea M. Fitzgerald. "But you can call me Miss Dorothea." She wore lipstick as bright as Red Skelton's hair. After she asked us a few questions, she led the four of us onto a stage, where we were seated side by side in white woven metal chairs. I spotted my mother and brother on bleachers in the crowded studio, where an expert whistler was warming up the audience by whistling the theme to channel nine's *Million Dollar Movie*.

The hot lights beat down on me; I heard a man counting down, "Five, four, three, two . . . " and around us the studio signs blinked *APPLAUSE*. The audience obeyed, clapping loudly as Art Linkletter dashed onto the stage. After he made some joke, he began asking the boy beside me some questions. Personal questions. And right then and there it sank in. Art Linkletter was going to ask questions of *me*, not of any other character or personality—but of *me*.

The audience laughed and clapped at the clever things the boy next to me said, and before I could even take a breath, Mr. Linkletter was kneeling by my chair, thrusting the microphone into my face.

I heard Dr. Troupe's words echoing through me: "Why do you want to be other people when you're such a fascinating young lady yourself?" but all my shyness washed over me, and I couldn't utter a word. Everything began to move in slow motion. I felt the bright heat of the lights on my head, the glare of the camera in my eyes, the mounting pressure in my chest as my heart pounded loudly and slowly, steady and hypnotic. And then, still in slow motion, I saw myself talking to Mr. Linkletter, but I couldn't hear a word I was saying—only a distorted facsimile of my voice, disembodied, out in the studio audience like some skilled ventriloquist's trick. I wanted to cry. I wanted to go home and pet my dog, Laddie. I felt as if my simple shift with the bouncy bow had vaporized into thin air, and I was completely naked onstage in front of millions.

As Mr. Linkletter stood, I snapped out of my trance. This was my last chance. I had to say something funny, or I'd be a big flop, and my life would be ruined. If I couldn't do it as me, then I'd call on one of my other personas—act as tough as the Girl from U.N.C.L.E., as spunky as Pollyanna, as carefree as Holly Golightly.

"Last question for you Hillary," Art said into the microphone. "What's your favorite thing your mom cooks?"

Out of nowhere, as if I were a medium channeling some ancient hayseed deity, I suddenly was Elly May Clampett from *The Beverly*

Hillbillies—thick Southern accent and all. "Well, Mr. Linkletter, she makes some mighty fine vittles—cooks up all sorts of critters!"

The audience went crazy. Art Linkletter was laughing so hard he had to wipe a tear from his eyes.

I did it. I was so relieved, I basked in the applause and smiled during the whole time the last two kids were interviewed. A man's voice announced parting gifts as a woman sauntered onstage and piled the items into our laps: a piece of Samsonite luggage, a watch, and an assortment of games—including Green Ghost, my favorite because it glowed in the dark.

Miss Dorothea whisked us off the stage and led us to a place called the commissary, where our chaperones met us. Mrs. Renzoli smiled at me, then said, "Good job, kid. Let's eat."

A large woman dressed in a white uniform, hair scrunched up in a hairnet, handed us orange speckled plastic trays and told us to help ourselves. I had been to Griswold's Smorgasbord off the 10 freeway with my parents, so I knew all about buffets. I began to pile food on my tray, selecting everything white or beige: mashed potatoes; macaroni and cheese; cottage cheese; tapioca pudding. I returned for several helpings, convinced everyone in the commissary—including Red Skelton, who had just walked in—was looking adoringly at me, too shy to ask for my autograph.

At home that night I sauntered into the kitchen, knowing my awaiting public would be there to greet me with cheers.

"HOWARD, STOP THAT RIGHT NOW!" My mother was yelling at my brother, who had shredded his white paper napkin into french fry-shaped strips and stuck them up his nose.

"I hate Salisbury steak," he screeched back. "I want Swiss steak!"

"You'll eat what your mother puts in front of you," my dad snapped.

I sat at the table and lay my napkin in my lap.

"Hey, Hill," Dad said, "Sorry I wasn't able to leave work and come to the show. How did it go?"

"Well, at first I was kinda shy—"

"Yeah, she sat there frozen, like a spazz!" Howard said, then threw a rolled-up piece of napkin at me.

"Nonsense, she was adorable," my mother chimed in.

Adorable? I started to perk up. "So then Mr. Linkletter asked me one more question—"

"Spazz," my brother interrupted.

"Would you let me finish?!" I turned back to my dad. "And, well, I made everyone laugh when I said—"

The phone rang. My mom answered it and told my dad it was Mrs. Goldman from up the street, who said he had offered to help her decide where to put her new furniture. "She wants to know if you can come by now."

My dad, a latent interior decorator, smiled. "Sure. Tell her I'll be right over."

I stood up and left the kitchen. I heard my dad calling, "Sorry, Hill. Tell me more when I get back?" As I walked up the stairs to my bedroom, I channeled Holly Golightly—English accent and all—whispering, "You don't have to worry. I've taken care of myself for a long time."

Again, for days I barely left my room. My mother forced me to go with her to Party Smarty, where she picked out colorful paper plates for one of her upcoming dinner parties, and every afternoon she insisted I ride my bike. Whenever she asked me what was wrong, I just said, "Nothing." How could I explain? At the end of the week, she walked into my room without knocking. "Nanny sent you something."

I lit up a bit, envisioning my grandmother who lived in Columbus, Ohio, sending me one of her famous packages of homemade cookies piled in layers of wax paper: thin, leaf-shaped shortbread, delicately covered in chocolate; butter cookies with dots of raspberry jam in the center. But my mother handed me an envelope. It was addressed to me in my grandmother's distinct, curly handwriting and was stamped DO NOT BEND. I opened it and found a stack of black-and-white photographs. Of Art Linkletter's *House Party*.

I looked closely at the snapshots. There seemed to have been some mix-up at the photo lab; my grandma had mistakenly sent pictures of some other girl from some other place and time. This girl was laughing—she even had a gleam in her eye.

As I studied the photographs, familiarity came into focus. I noticed the striped shift with the white Peter Pan collar and bouncy bow, the forehead fringed with messy bangs. I began to recognize who that child was. It wasn't Elly May Clampett, Pollyanna, or even Holly Golightly. It was the little girl Dr. Troupe found fascinating. It was me.

1968

✳ Even though Helen Keller dies, my fellow sixth-graders and I continue telling Helen Keller jokes. One of my favorites: What did Helen Keller's parents do to punish her for swearing? Washed her hands with soap.

✳ I win first place at a "Hat Day" contest at my elementary school with a hat I made from a birdcage. Years later, I'll see Anaïs Nin wearing a birdcage hat in the experimental film *Inauguration of the Pleasure Dome*.

✳ After delivering his "mountaintop" speech, Martin Luther King Jr. is assassinated. Riots break out in more than one hundred cities.

✳ My cousin, a college freshman, is one of the protesters who seize the administration building at Trinity College in Hartford, Connecticut, and hold the trustees hostage, demanding scholarships for African Americans. Just days later, student protesters at New York's Columbia University take over the administration building and shut down the university for a week, causing police to storm the campus and violently remove the students and their supporters.

✳ Yippies are at the center of massive anti-war demonstrations at the Chicago Democratic National Convention.

* *Apollo 8* astronauts, the first humans to see the far side of the Moon and planet Earth as a whole, carry Silly Putty into space to alleviate boredom and, during weightlessness, use it to help fasten down tools. Meanwhile I'm busy using Silly Putty to lift impressions off my Archie, Dot, and Little Lotta comic books.

* Moments after declaring victory in the California Democratic presidential primary, Sen. Robert F. Kennedy is assassinated at the Ambassador Hotel.

* My friend Ava Atkins and I make love beads, then set up a stand to sell them on her street—busy Sunset Boulevard, where no cars can stop.

* I am crushed when the final episode of *The Monkees* airs but manage to perk up when two new groovy shows debut: *Rowan and Martin's Laugh-In* and *The Mod Squad*.

Mrs. Paul Henreid's Trrophhhy Baaallll

When my progressive, liberal parents announced that I would be attending cotillion, I was sure they had lost their minds. Well, that was after they explained to me what cotillion even *was*, since in all my eleven years I had never before heard the word.

"Dance classes," my mom said, as she cleared our empty TV dinner trays off the table. "It's in a ballroom at the Beverly Hilton Hotel, and you get all dressed up. You even get to wear gloves."

"Really?" I said, trying to contain my excitement. I appreciated that my parents would allow me to wear gloves again, considering the last time I did, I'd been suspended from the third grade.

But it made sense. My parents were always trying to convince me to wear more girlie things—well, actually *anything* other than my jeans and Monkees sweatshirt.

"It's not just any cotillion, it's Mrs. Paul Henreid's," my mom added, like I wasn't already sold on the idea.

"Who's that?"

"Paul Henreid's a well-known actor," my dad said, putting down his newspaper. "He did a famous scene in the movie *Now, Voyager* where he lights two cigarettes at one time."

"Neat."

"Your friends Ava and Karen are going, too," Mom said as she put down a plate of Ding Dongs and Ring Dings. Could life get any better?

"When do I start?"

It was one long week before cotillion began. After school on Wednesday, Ava's mom dropped the three of us off at the Beverly Hilton Hotel. We walked into the chandeliered ballroom, where it looked like all the white-gloved girls were attending an antibacteria convention. As usual, I was underdressed. While the other girls were clad in fancy white frocks—some with tulle that looked like atomic mushroom clouds—I wore a beige wool dress embroidered with psychedelic hippie flowers.

An older woman with two slashes of dark brown lipstick between her nose and chin welcomed us all in a thick, indistinguishable accent. "I am Mrs. Paul Henreid, and we're so veddy happy to have you here wid us. I would like to introduce you to your teachah, my partnah, Mrs. Marie Sawyer."

A glamorous lady with an exotic poof of hair sculpted together with an entire can of Aqua Net, strolled gracefully to the middle of the vast ballroom. I had only seen hair like hers on mannequins at Bullocks department store.

"Welcome, young ladies and gentlemen. In cotillion we will teach you not only ballroom dancing but also proper manners and etiquette." I felt pools of sweat forming in my armpits, and my wool hippie dress began to itch. "In our weeks together, you will learn how to curtsy and bow as well as fox-trot, waltz, tango, and cha-cha, all leading up to our ... " she paused for effect, her manner creating a silent drum roll, " ... *grand Trophy Ball!*"

A murmur of excitement swept the room. It was at this point I noticed in the corner an adorable boy with blond hair and dreamy blue eyes. He looked familiar but I couldn't place him.

"Today we will begin with the cha-cha," Mrs. Marie Sawyer said. "Boys, please form a line on one side, girls on the other."

We stepped into our lines, and as I took my place next to Ava and

Karen, I heard a few of the girls whispering. They motioned toward the boy with the dreamy blue eyes. "That's Darby Hinton," a girl in shiny patent leather shoes said.

"Who?" another girl with long, braided hair whispered back.

"He plays the son on the TV show *Daniel Boone*. I want him for my partner."

The word startled me. Partner? We would dance with partners? Of course, that's why the two lines. Well, if that were the case, then I wanted blue eyes to be *my* partner—I spotted him first, even *before* I knew he was Daniel Boone's son.

Mrs. Sawyer stepped between the lines. "Before we begin, I would like you all to introduce yourselves. Ladies first."

One by one, thirty girls in white gloves announced their names, giving me time to check everyone out. Two girls, Jamie and Kelly, said they were sisters. I remembered their names because I thought one day I'd like to be just like them—bubbly and jazzy. Also, it was hard not to notice that Kelly had the same dreamy eyes as the *Daniel Boone* boy. Too bad *she* couldn't be my partner.

After the boys introduced themselves, Mrs. Sawyer chimed in, "I would also like you to meet the TAs—teacher's assistants." She introduced three teen girls, whose names I missed, and then the teen boy TAs—Jacques, an exotic foreigner; Scott, who wore a stylish turtleneck; and Corbin, a handsome blond teenager whose last name was Bernsen and who years later would star on *L.A. Law*. The TAs waved at us.

"Now boys," Mrs. Sawyer said as she turned to the line of eleven-year-olds, "each of you please pick a partner."

It was a smorgasbord of possibilities. Though my first choice was Kelly, I would be happy with Daniel Boone Jr. or any of the older TAs. I nonchalantly flipped my short hair back, waiting to see who'd whisk me away first.

Darby Hinton headed toward me but walked right past and went up to the bouncy sisters, offering his hand to Kelly. Darn. Two down.

I stood still and watched as boys sauntered over, picking one, then another, then another girl. When the handsome boy TAs veered in my direction, I felt my skin grow hot. But they passed me by and asked Ava and Karen to dance. One by one pairs strolled off. And then I realized the horrible truth: *I was the only girl left standing in the line.* My heart sank. The remaining boy, the fattest boy, the boy who kept wiping his sweaty hands down the legs of his black suit pants, waddled over and put his arm out toward me. I hesitantly linked my arm through his and smiled an exaggerated, overcompensating smile, swallowing hard so that I wouldn't cry.

Mrs. Sawyer began to lead the class in the cha-cha, and my two friends demonstrated steps with their handsome TA partners.

"One, two, cha-cha-cha. Three, four, cha-cha-cha."

I felt awash in shame. I cha'd where I should have *cha'd,* stepped forward when I should have stepped back, and by the time everyone else seemed to have caught on, I was actually glad my partner was the loser boy—at least I didn't mind stepping on his feet.

"Lovely, lovely," Mrs. Sawyer cooed over everyone's performance except for mine and my partner's. "This will be one of the competitions at the Trophy Ball!" she chimed in an exaggerated fashion— Trrophhhy Baaallll. "So be sure to practice at home. Five, six, cha-cha-cha."

When I arrived home that night and we all sat down to dinner, I begged my parents to let me quit.

"You were so excited about it," my mother said, holding on to a tray of hot Tater Tots with a large, plaid oven mitt. "What happened?"

"Nothing happened," I answered defensively. "It was just stupid. When am I ever going to need to curtsy or cha-cha? I'm not going back."

For the next week, we had the same conversation nightly, while my brother drummed Beatles tunes on the table with his fork and knife, and my dad kept shushing him. Dad didn't even care about cotillion, except for the fact that they had already paid for it. Mom, however, was adamant. "It'll get better," she kept saying, "just give it more time."

It didn't get better. In fact, it only got worse. Week after week I was the fat loser stuck with the fat loser boy, and my two winner friends danced with the winner TAs. I tripped doing the fox-trot, slipped doing the waltz, and when I was dipped during the tango, I prayed that my partner's sweaty hands would lose their grip and I would drop to the floor cracking enough vertebrae to ensure I would never be able to dance again. No such luck.

And if I wasn't miserable enough, each week Mrs. Sawyer reminded us again and again about the upcoming Trrophhhy Baaallll.

"It'll be a star-studded night," she'd say with a gleam in her eye.

I couldn't imagine why any stars would want to come watch some lame dance contest featuring a bunch of eleven-year-olds.

The afternoon of the ball, I pretended I was sick so I didn't have to go be humiliated in front of even more people, including my own parents. "So, I guess I'll just have to miss it," I croaked to my dad, feigning disappointment.

He didn't buy it. "Come on, it'll be fun," he said.

"Fun? I'd rather eat shards of glass."

When my parents and I arrived at the Beverly Hilton Hotel and parked in the self-park garage, we saw a line of limousines snaking in front of the entrance. Signs in ornate calligraphy pointed the way to Mrs. Paul Henreid's Trophy Ball in the Grand Ballroom, which I discovered was much larger than the less-grand ballroom we had used for class each week. Round tables with white tablecloths and elegant bouquet centerpieces were arranged to face the dance floor. The silverware and crystal on the tables gleamed under the chandeliers.

We sat with the Atkinses and the Spences at a table across from the table where sisters Kelly and Jamie sat. When I looked at their mother, I felt this weird shiver crawl up my spine, and I had no idea why until Mrs. Atkins leaned toward my mom and dad and whispered in her Southern lilt, "Can you believe we're sitting so close to Janet Leigh?"

No wonder I was creeped out. The last time I'd seen Kelly and Jamie Lee Curtis's mom, it was on TV in a movie my babysitter had let me watch as long as I didn't tell my parents—*a movie where she was naked and being stabbed to death in a shower.*

"And look over there," Mrs. Spence chimed in, pointing to another table where a few of my classmates sat. "Michael Landon, Vincent Price, and Charlton Heston."

"And there's Jack Benny!" my mother yelped giddily.

I finally understood why Mrs. Sawyer kept saying the night would be "star-studded." The stars studding the event were my classmates' *parents.*

Dad was leafing through the souvenir program placed on each plate. I peered over his shoulder and read the inside cover: "Guests of Honor—All Our Fathers," and a list titled "Patrons and Patronesses." Mr. and Mrs. Atkins were first on the list. I was trying to locate our name when suddenly I saw my dad's bottom lip begin to curl. This only happened when he was really mad—like when we were at the Palm Springs 31 Flavors and the ice cream guy didn't pack my Jamoca Almond Fudge tightly enough on my cone and, at first lick, the scoop fell onto the sidewalk, and then the guy wouldn't fix it *or* give us our money back.

Dad elbowed Mom. Her finger traced the list, moving down the alphabet to the Cs. I could tell by the look on her face that our name was not on the list.

Oh no. I slinked down in my chair. Would my father get up and brazenly demand the wrong be righted just as he had at 31 Flavors? Would he embarrass me more than I already was? Was that even possible?

Thankfully, just in time to distract my father, Mrs. Paul Henreid, who hadn't appeared since our very first class, strolled to a podium and leaned into a microphone that squealed with feedback. "Good evening Ladies und Gentlemen. I am honored to welcome you to Mrs. Paul Henreid's Cotillion Trophy Ball of 1968!"

I sneaked a peek at my dad, who was now lighting a cigarette and sucking on it with his still-curled lip.

"I would like to introduce you to my husband, Paul Henreid." The actor joined his wife at the podium, then began to speak. But I wasn't listening. I was too busy concentrating on my father, wondering if now it would be him, instead of Paul Henreid, lighting up two cigarettes at one time.

Then Mrs. Henreid introduced Mrs. Marie Sawyer, who clapped her hands together and said, "Let the competition begin."

The first dance she announced was the fox-trot. Crap. This was the one category I'd been assigned to compete in. My fat, sweaty partner approached with extended arm. I looked away from my parents so I wouldn't see the disappointment on their faces.

Once on the floor, I curtsied; my partner bowed. There was no turning back now. We began, and while twenty young couples danced, several judges walked through, staring at our feet, our arms, our torsos, studying our every move.

My partner and I fox-trotted—or at least we attempted some unrecognizable semblance of what had once been considered the ballroom dance. After three excruciating minutes the music finally ended, and we all sat down. The parents clapped as enthusiastically as they could while maintaining their requisite Beverly Hills' reserve.

The judges then moved to the podium and whispered to Mrs. Sawyer, who called out the names of the first-, second-, and third-place winners. Hmmm. Fascinating coincidence. Every winning couple included a child of a celebrity. Flashbulbs popped as the winners returned to the dance floor to receive their trophies.

I could finally take a breath. I had served my sentence, and in just an hour or so, I would be a free woman/girl. I could go back to my bike-riding, hill-climbing, Monkees sweatshirt-wearing days. The eight agonizing, humiliating, soul-crushing weeks of cotillion were almost over.

I dived into my cup of what the program called "Supreme of Fresh Fruit Princesse" and ate every bite. I glanced at the back of the program and read another list of people who "sponsored or presented trophies from 1958–1968 and their sons and daughters." Eddie Albert, Lloyd Bridges, James Garner, Bob Hope, Jerry Lewis, Karl Malden, Jack Palance, Maureen O'Hara, Robert Wagner, and Natalie Wood.

What the hell were we doing here? My dad ran a baby furniture business. He had met my mom in Columbus, Ohio. The only stars I had ever seen in person were at the corner market: Miss Jane Hathaway, buying meatballs; and Alfred Hitchcock, who I overheard asking for his favorite ice cream, "Vanillllllllla."

Thank God it was almost over.

The next two competition categories were the waltz and the tango. As more celebrities' children won trophies, the rumbling at our table grew deeper and more pronounced. I personally had never expected to win, place, or even show, but Ava and Karen had. And clearly other "ordinary" children *and their parents* had as well.

The displeasure was not restricted to our table, and I could feel the tension in the room grow as thick as Mrs. Marie Sawyer's hairspray. I felt like we were in *West Side Story*—the Curtis/Leigh, Heston, Price, and Landon kids were the Sharks, and the rest of the just-plain folks, the Jets. And I didn't even figure into this dance-off. I was the tomboy, Anybodys. Or, more aptly, *Nobodys*. By the time the cha-cha competition ended and Jack Benny's grandson won first place—Mrs. Atkins blurting, "But he can't even dance!"—I was sure I was going to see an uprising. And judging by my father's lip, which was by now so curled it completely obscured his mouth and made him look like a sideshow freak, I knew who would be leading the rebellion. I just didn't know *how*. I couldn't decide whether to excuse myself and hide out in the ladies room or stay and try to calm my father down.

Then Mrs. Marie Sawyer leaned into the microphone. "We have one last competition not listed in your souvenir program. In honor of tonight's theme, we have a surprise category called the Father/Daughter Freestyle! Fathers, daughters, hit the floor, it's time to dance!"

"Come on," my dad snapped, grabbing my gloved hand. "We'll show them all."

Oh. No.

He dragged me to the dance floor and started to let loose. And I mean *loose*. Dad was not dancing the way the stars or even the Beverly Hills socialites danced. My dad was *feeling* the music. Eyes closed, he began to gyrate and spin, offering up interpretive dance moves as if he were listening to the Rolling Stones instead of Tony Bennett. Dancing with abandon, fingers snapping, arms flailing to the beat, he was groovy, man.

I looked up and saw everyone staring at us. The Hestons. The Landons. Even Janet Leigh. A few people pointed. Some laughed.

Then suddenly, the dancers on the floor stepped aside—just the way they did on *American Bandstand* when a featured dancer began doing some killer moves. My father twirled me into the middle like I was one of the *Jackie Gleason Show*'s June Taylor Dancers. I did my best to keep up with him, but there was no hope. Despite my total ineptitude, my father's carefree attitude seemed to be infectious. People began to clap along. I was so utterly mortified, I was ready to fling myself off a balcony into the deep end of the Beverly Hilton swimming pool. I swore then and there that I would never speak to my father again. *Never.*

The song finally ended. My dad's lip had unfurled, and he was smiling, in his glory, as the crowd went wild with applause.

"Well, wasn't that something?" Mrs. Sawyer called out over the microphone. The judges whispered in her ear, and she announced, "I guess there's no question who wins first-prize trophy for the Father Daughter Freestyle dance. Hillary Carlip and her father, Bob Carlip, congratulations!"

I floated out of my body. Instead of standing in the spotlight of attention, I imagined myself sitting next to my first choice for a partner, Kelly Curtis, casually sipping Shirley Temples, laughing and discussing how embarrassing parents can be.

Flashbulbs popped, bringing me back. And there I was, holding a trophy. *Me.* My father gripped my other hand and held it high in the air. And I let him. I smiled at Dad, sharing our victory.

As Mrs. Henreid and Mrs. Sawyer bid everyone "Adieu, till next year," classmates came up to me saying things like, "Wow!" and "That was something!" My fat, sweaty partner put out his hand to shake mine. "Thanks, you really showed them all." And then Darby Hinton came up to me, too. "That was really cool."

Not only had my dad saved the day for the everyman and everywoman in the room that night, he had also upped my credibility. Maybe, I thought, I'd never again be the one picked last. Maybe now I would dance with a handsome TA or a dreamy child star. Maybe I could even have a say in things and insist, "Girls and girls or boys and boys can dance together."

But wait a minute . . . if I wanted all that, I'd have to come back to cotillion next year. Well, I thought, as we drove home into the suddenly sweet night, if someone has to kick the Goulets' and Montalbans' asses, it might as well be me.

Mrs. Paul Henreid's

Trophy Ball

in Association with

Mrs. Marie Sawyer

1968

Jamie Curtis

Kelly Curtis

Hillary Carlip

Corbin Bernson

THE BIG MOMENT

Young People Receive Trophies For Dance Achievement

Cesar Romero
Berry
Polly
Michael Landon
Becca
Dean Jones

Jimmy Dean
Jim Backus
Charlton Heston
Rick Jason
Janet Leigh
Karl Malden

Spring 1971

* Though Happy Face buttons hit their peak of popularity with more than fifty million sold, the button I wear says: "Impeach Tricky Dick."

* I hang out with my good friend Brina Gehry at her cookie-cutter, suburban home in Westwood while her father, Frank, is off working—though I don't even know what he does for a living.

* Most kids in my school wear Frye boots, gauchos, ponchos, and puka shells. I wear peasant blouses, army jackets, Earth Shoes, and a halter top I make out of an American flag, which provokes many strangers on the street to scream at me, calling me unpatriotic.

✻ My working mother discovers the newly introduced Hamburger Helper and couldn't be more thrilled.

✻ At a Grateful Dead concert in San Francisco, more than thirty fans go to the hospital after unknowingly drinking apple juice laced with LSD. Meanwhile, I smoke a joint with a friend that we find out later was laced with PCP, and I end up passed out in an alley, hallucinating the head of my dead grandfather, whom I never met, flying around on wings.

✻ After he's my classmate for a short stint at Emerson Junior High, Michael Jackson has his first solo hit single, "Got to Be There."

They're Very Loyal Fans, and They Bake

Music helped drown out the dissonance of my adolescence. I'd climb out to the roof from my second-story bedroom window and blast Cat Stevens's "Wild World" so I wouldn't have to hear my brother constantly arguing with my parents. I'd listen to Laura Nyro's "Lonely Women" so I would stop thinking about the boys who didn't like me, and to Joni Mitchell's "I Don't Know Where I Stand" to forget the twenty-two pounds I lost and had rapidly gained back, plus ten.

After a while, the records weren't enough. That's when I began frequenting the Troubadour, the hottest nightclub in seventies L.A.

The "Troub," as we regulars called it, was an intimate joint where the great singer-songwriters performed two shows a night, six nights a week. I saw Joni Mitchell, Bonnie Raitt, James Taylor, Laura Nyro, and even Elton John, whose sweat dripped onto my arm as I watched from a table right under the stage. It didn't matter that I was only fourteen years old—no one at the Troub ever checked IDs.

One warm April night, the scent of honeysuckle drenching the air, my friend Molly and I hitchhiked to the Troub to hear Cat Stevens. First in line, I caught my reflection in the window of the martial arts studio next door to the club. Dressed in my favorite thrift store outfit—embroidered peasant blouse, patched bell-bottom jeans, and a long fifties-style blue wool coat that I rarely took off—I actually felt uncharacteristically attractive. Well, until I spotted Molly's reflection next to me—blonder, a foot taller, and much shapelier in a halter top than I.

Once inside the club Molly and I grabbed one of the front tables, ordered bubbly ginger ales, and sipped them through pink cocktail straws. Nobody, including us, had ever heard of the opening act—a lanky, tall woman who sauntered onto the stage with a guitar, followed by her backup band, three guys with a lot of hair.

An announcer spoke over the PA. "Ladies and gentlemen, please give a warm welcome to new Elektra recording artist, Miss Carly Simon."

The singer's voice was rich, deep, and intoxicating, her smile so broad it lit up like an angelic jack-o'-lantern. I knew immediately that this woman was different from all the other girl singers. Her lyrics were defiant: *"You say we'll soar like two birds through the clouds, but soon you'll cage me on your shelf. I'll never learn to be just me first, by myself."* I had goose bumps. Carly captivated me. I knew I had to return for the next five nights. I knew I would meet Carly Simon. No, I wouldn't just meet her.

I would befriend Carly Simon.

When the show was over and we were filing out of the club, the only teenagers in a sea of adults, I grabbed Molly's arm. "Come on," I whispered, dragging her up a set of narrow, carpeted stairs. Without question Molly followed, playing Ethel to my Lucy.

At the top of the stairs, I found what I was looking for: Taped to one of two paint-splattered doors was a yellow scrap of paper with Carly's name scrawled on it in ballpoint pen.

I knocked tentatively.

The door swung open, and there she stood, towering over me, tall and graceful, wearing a long paisley dress and brown lace-up boots. "Yes?" she asked in that lush, resonant voice.

I nearly fell over backwards. "Uh, hi. We just wanted to tell you how amazingly talented you are." Shit. That sounded stupid—like something a *fan* would say.

I quickly added, "And you're a true artist."

Much better. Weightier.

Carly beamed. "Well, thank you. You girls want to come in?"

"Sure," I stuttered, surprised by the invitation—especially after my lame opening.

We stepped into clouds of cigarette smoke that nearly obscured our view of the three band members crammed into the tiny space. The pianist, a skinny man with a ponytail that spilled down his back, moved over to make room for us on a ratty, plaid couch. We squeezed in between him and the drummer, who was dabbing his damp head full of curls with a paper towel. "So, you guys like the show?" he asked.

"Are you kidding? It was fantastic," I yipped, then toned it down. "You're all very talented."

"Yeah," Molly added.

Carly looked right at me. "I want to know what you *really* think. Good or bad. Be honest."

Oh my God. Someone wanted to know what I *really* thought. I had better come up with something good. "Well . . . " I began hesitantly, "your songs are moving, your voice gorgeous, and the band's fantastic. My only criticism is that it's hard to hear your voice on some of the more upbeat songs. Maybe they need to turn up your vocal mic?"

Carly smiled, those full lips spreading across her face. "Excellent point. So, do you girls go to a lot of concerts? What kinds of music do you like?"

I was blown away. Most adults asked the same idiotic questions: How old are you? What's your favorite subject in school? What do you want to be when you grow up? But not my new friend Carly.

"I like female singer-songwriters. Joni Mitchell, Laura Nyro."

"Janis Joplin," Molly added.

"You guys have great taste," Carly said, smiling that smile again.

We hung out for more than a half hour, chatting with Carly and the band. When the guitarist with the muttonchop sideburns began to organize his gear for the second set, we stood up to leave. "We gonna see you again this week?" he asked.

"Sure, definitely." I said.

"Definitely," Molly echoed.

"Good," Carly said.

It was a solid good. Like she meant it. Then, at the door, Carly Simon *hugged* me.

We floated out of the club and onto Santa Monica Boulevard, nonchalantly walking past the martial arts studio, then across Doheny. It wasn't until we reached a small, secluded park where we were certain no one could see or hear us that we both finally let loose our screams.

"Oh. My. God. That was surreal!" I slalomed through a line of trees, then flopped onto the grass and rolled around in circles.

"I can't believe you just knocked on her door," Molly shouted, "and that she invited us in!"

"Watch," I said, "she's gonna be a huge star. I just know it."

I didn't want to go home yet, back to my solitary bedroom, my ordinary existence where no one asked questions that mattered.

The next day, trapped in my beige stucco junior high school, I couldn't concentrate. I kept replaying the night before, anticipating what would happen *this* night. How excited Carly would be to see me. How we'd sit on the couch together, talking about music, art, literature, philosophy.

Yeah, right. Who was I kidding? Why would Carly Simon want to be my friend? I would have to win her over.

The minute I got home from school, I baked banana bread as an offering for Carly and the band. That evening we arrived early at the Troub and snagged our front row table. All through the first set I held the still-warm loaf in my lap, as protectively as if it were a newborn.

At intermission, Molly and I hurried upstairs. When Carly opened the door, she grinned, and the guitarist called out, "Hey, it's the girls!"

The girls. We were *the girls*.

I handed Carly the banana bread. She thanked me and placed it on the coffee table, next to an overflowing ashtray, and the guys immediately dug in.

"Did you notice we cranked up the vocals on the up-tempo songs?" Carly asked. "Great suggestion last night, Hillary."

I suppressed the squeal rising in my throat. "You sounded incredible."

I had recently added the words "incredible" and "amazing" to my vocabulary because my friend Amy's older sister said them, and she was cool—she had a black boyfriend who played the flute.

While Cat Stevens performed downstairs, we sat on the couch joining in the conversation as Carly and the band dissected their show. When we heard the applause at the end of Cat's first set, I stood.

"Sorry we can't stay, but we'll see you tomorrow night."

The band waved, thanking us for the bread. And this time at the door, Carly Simon *kissed* me good-bye.

All that week, bringing gifts of pumpkin, date-nut, cinnamon-raisin, and honey-walnut breads, recipes courtesy of *The Tassajara Bread Book*, Molly and I hung out in Carly's dressing room. On the third night, she added us to the guest list—a great relief, since with the $4.00 ticket price and the cost of baking ingredients, my weekly allowance was hardly enough to keep up.

On closing night, when Cat Stevens ended his set, we knew the time to say good-bye had come. My eyes welled up with tears, but I bit my lip and held them back. Be strong. *Be strong*.

"Well," I said as I headed to the door, "it was great hanging out with you guys."

"Yeah," Molly added. "Thanks for getting us in and all."

Carly stood. As she leaned over to give us the good-bye hug and kiss we'd grown accustomed to, she said, "Next time I'm back, you promise to come see me?"

Was she kidding? Of course we'd come see her. What were friends for?

The next seven months dragged, the only high point being news of Carly's success. "That's the Way I've Always Heard It Should Be," a song from her first album, rose on the charts, and just as she released her second album, *Anticipation*, we learned she was returning to the Troub. This time as the headliner.

On a rainy November opening night, armed with a loaf of three-layer corn bread, Molly and I opted for a table in the back so we could unobtrusively leave our seats during the opening act and visit Carly upstairs. A singer-songwriter named Don McLean was onstage, performing a new song called "American Pie," when Molly and I crept to the dressing room. My heart was beating faster and harder than it had the first time I knocked on that door. After all, Carly was a star now. What if she wasn't as welcoming as before? Worse, what if she'd forgotten us?

I took a deep breath and knocked.

The door opened a crack and a man in a dark suit gruffly said, "Yes?"

"Uh, we're here to say hi to Carly and give her this," I said, holding out the loaf.

"She can't see anyone now," he snapped, obviously thinking we were just some *fans*. He started to close the door on us, but I stuck my foot inside and shouted, "Tell her it's Hillary and Molly!"

In an instant, Carly appeared at the door.

"It's the girls!" she cried, and she hugged and kissed us as if those seven months had only been a moment.

She was, truly, our friend.

So again Molly and I spent a week hanging out with Carly and the band. One night, between songs, Carly looked out at the audience and said, "This one is for Hillary and Molly," then launched into "Anticipation." The next night she dedicated "One More Time," and every night after that, Carly dedicated a song to us.

I had never before felt so happy. So important.

Hillary Carlip

Months passed. It was on an overly smoggy summer day, at a news-stand in Westwood Village, that I spotted an interview with Carly in *Where It's At*, a popular music magazine. I began to read, when suddenly my heart nearly stopped.

"'At the Troubadour, it's been great,'" Carly was quoted. "'There are these two girls who have really just made my evenings there.'"

Fuckin' A! Carly was talking about me and Molly. In a magazine!

I threw money down on the counter, grabbed the magazine, and raced five blocks to Molly's house. I arrived sweating and gasping heavily. "There's an interview in . . . Carly . . . mentions us."

Molly snatched the magazine and began to read aloud.

"'At the Troubadour, it's been great. There are these two girls who have really just made my evenings there.'"

"Can you believe it?" I yelled, loud enough for the neighbors to hear. The poodle next door began to yip.

"'They've been sitting in the front row every night. They come to all the shows and they bake me bread, and they sing along.'"

"Amazing," I screeched, then grabbed the magazine from Molly. I continued reading. "'They know all the songs and, as many times as they've heard them, when I start them, they say, "Oh, great!" It's really exciting to have such great . . .'"

I stopped midsentence.

"Such great what?" Molly barked.

I was devastated. Stunned into silence.

Molly grabbed the magazine from me and read. "'It's really exciting to have such great fans.'" She closed the magazine and looked at me. "What's wrong?"

After a moment, I finally said, "*Fans.* She called us *fans.*"

"Oh." Molly paused. "Well, she called us *great* fans. And she also said a lot of other cool things about us."

"I thought we were friends."

I left Molly's house and trudged home. There I locked myself in my room, where I ate an entire still-frozen Sara Lee pound cake and listened to records—anyone but Carly. The words "such great fans" echoed through my head, replacing previous insults classmates had heaped upon me. "Fat ass." "Lezzie."

After four days I knew what I had to do. If Carly were truly my friend, she would understand why I had to write. I composed ten drafts of a letter before settling on the final version, which I then re-read twenty times.

Dear Carly:

We saw your interview in Where It's At *and have to say, were very disappointed. We were surprised to be thrown into the category of "fans" with so many others who, I'm sure, you appreciate, but, well—we just thought we were more. We thought we were friends. I guess we were wrong. If we're wrong about being wrong, please write back. We still think you're a very talented woman.*

Hillary and Molly

I jumped on my bike, rode to the corner mailbox, and dropped in the letter before I could change my mind.

Every day after school I waited in the driveway for Felix, our mailman, and every day he shook his head and said, "Sorry, nothing for you today. You waiting for grades? An invitation to a bar mitzvah?"

"No, Felix," I said brusquely, not bothering to give him any more information, since he clearly didn't get me.

Finally, after two weeks of disappointment, Felix drove up holding a powder blue envelope with my name written on it in neat, loopy handwriting.

"This what you've been waiting for?" he asked, handing me the envelope.

"Yes!" I squealed. I tore into the house then upstairs to my room and closed the door. Sitting on my twin bed, I carefully opened the envelope and inhaled the patchouli oil that wafted up from the stationery. The letter was handwritten:

Dear Hell + Molly

Don't believe everything you read! I don't usually use the word "fans" but I can understand your being offended. No of course I don't think of you as that! But if I started to defend myself against the words that interviewers put in my mouth I wouldn't have time to write anymore songs or even clean my house.

I am well! I've come back from Hawaii with a subtle tan and an unsubtle case of sun poisoning — but the vacation was great and I'm back to work tomorrow. I'll be at the Troubadour May 2. Please come! I'm looking forward to seeing you —

Love,
Carly

I sat on my bed, unable to hold back tears of relief and joy. Just then, my brother barged into the room without knocking.

"GET OUT!!!!!!!" I screamed so loudly he jumped, then slammed the door.

I put on a Carly record and turned up the volume, singing "The

Love's Still Growing" along with her while I tucked the letter safely inside my shirt and pressed it to my skin.

In early May, Molly and I returned to the Troub. Carly was a huge star by then. Even though she'd won a Grammy for Best New Artist, free tickets still awaited us, and the front table was reserved for us at every show. After the performances, we hung out in the dressing room that had become so familiar I knew every stain on that plaid couch.

On closing night I brought along a clunky tape recorder that I held on my lap during the show. It was a perfect performance to tape because just as Carly was about to sing "Summer's Coming Around Again," my favorite song, she leaned into the microphone and said:

> *"This song is dedicated to Hillary and Molly, who have been in the front seats of this club more times this week than I have. They're very loyal fans, and they bake. You should meet them, because if they like you, they're a powerful, powerful duo."*

What stands out on the tape over Carly's voice is held-back, breathy, fourteen-year-old excitement escaping from me in short, giddy giggles. I was so high from her lengthy dedication and her hearty hug and kiss good-bye, it wasn't until I returned home well after midnight and played the tape that I heard the word.

Fans.

She called us fans.

Still, when I climbed out my bedroom window and crawled onto the roof, I played the tape over and over again. Sitting beneath a dim crescent moon, I didn't mind anymore. Was Carly leaving free tickets and reserving front-row seats for anyone else? Who was she mentioning in interviews, writing letters to, dedicating songs to, and calling powerful? Who did she invite up to her dressing room every night and not only ask for opinions but listen to them as if they counted? And who was the one who had made it all happen?

Hillary Carlip

Me.

I turned up the tape recorder, looked at the Moon, and let Carly's lyrics seep into my being, my every cell.

"We want you to love the world, to know it well and play a part. And we'll help you to learn to love yourself 'cause that's where lovin' really starts."

Summer 1971

* I go downtown to watch a Black Panther trial and wind up talking to the Manson girls, who hold a daily vigil for Charlie outside the courthouse. I can't help but stare at the *X*s carved crudely in their foreheads and admire the playing card designs they embroider on muslin.

* I cut my hair to look like Jane Fonda in *Klute* but instead end up looking like Keith Partridge.

* Although cigarette ads are banned on TV, my father doesn't quit his three-pack-a-day habit. He chain-smokes all the way through *Marcus Welby, M.D.* and *Medical Center*.

* *Apollo 15* carries the first men to drive on the Moon in the Lunar Rover. I go on a crash diet and eat only Space Food Sticks: butterscotch for breakfast, peanut butter for lunch, and chocolate for dinner.

* The Twenty-Sixth Amendment to the U.S. Constitution lowers the voting age from twenty-one to eighteen. Good news, but at fourteen, I still have four years to go before I can vote, and I can't wait—especially after the Pentagon Papers are leaked.

* I see snow for the first time—at the top of the tram in Palm Springs!

✳ Jim Morrison ODs in Paris. Because Jimi Hendrix and Janis Joplin have recently died, some fans believe all three are alive and in hiding or have been assassinated by an anti-rock conspiracy. I'm still convinced Paul McCartney is dead and continue to gather clues for proof.

✳ *Steal This Book*, by yippie Abbie Hoffman, is released. My best friend, Greg, and I join in "challenging the status quo" by going to Figaro's restaurant, ordering a huge amount of food on one check and two Cokes on a separate check, then going up to the cashier and paying only the check for the Cokes. Right on.

✳ While songs like "One Less Bell to Answer," "Gypsies, Tramps, and Thieves," and "I'd Like to Teach the World to Sing" are in the top ten, I know every lyric on every Joni Mitchell album and "fill my drawing book with line" so I can be like Trina, one of Joni's "Ladies of the Canyon."

The King Case

I knew I had found a kindred spirit in Greg when we were in the seventh grade and bonded over Bea Benaderet. After a rousing game of spin the bottle, complete with closed-mouth kissing, our party host, Melanie Morgan, turned off all the lights in her den and lit a candle, creating an eerie mood for a séance.

"Let's bring back JFK," Melanie suggested to the twelve of us sitting in a circle around the candle.

"We always do JFK," Ricky Marx said. "Let's contact Marilyn Monroe!"

And then as if we had rehearsed the moment, Greg and I simultaneously said, "How about Bea Benaderet?"

"Who?" Everyone else in the room turned and looked at us like we were freaks.

"The actress from *Petticoat Junction*," I explained.

"She just died yesterday," Greg added.

It was the start of a long friendship.

A cross between David Bowie and Albert Einstein, Greg's thick nest of dark blond hair hung well past his shoulders, making him appear much older than his thirteen years. When he spoke he drew out each word in singsongy precision. He called me "Doll," but it was more like "Dolllllllllllllll." He was obviously gay, a fact his parents were made painfully aware of when, at the age of three, he took to wearing his mother's pearls. Although I hadn't yet realized that I, too, was gay, it was clear in our relationship who wore the pants.

Greg and I shared a passion for the unconventional and eccentric. We devoured *Grapefruit*, Yoko Ono's book of "happenings," and created our own "events," constantly daring each other to do random, outlandish things in public—like the time when we were walking out of the Ahmanson Theatre, after seeing Richard Chamberlain in *Night of the Iguana*, and Greg gave me a dare that, of course, I had to fulfill. Amid the stylish post-theater crowd, I strolled across the busy downtown street, subtly untied my wrap-around skirt, and let it fall to the ground, pretending not to notice. I walked for three blocks in only my underwear.

Greg and I also shared a love of music—the more obscure, the better. Together we discovered performers like the jazz vocal group Lambert, Hendricks, and Ross, who scatted their way through "Halloween Spooks," and Frances Faye, featuring Jack Costanzo on bongos, whose album we bought simply because we liked her short, snazzy haircut and the liner notes that stated she lived in Hollywood with her "secretary and four French poodles."

One night in late November, Greg and I went to the Troub to see James Taylor. But, once again, I was even more blown away by James's opening act. This singer's résumé of songs she had written for other artists was amazing, and now she was striking out on her own. Her name was Carole King.

Something about Carole moved me beyond the feelings I had for other performers I'd seen—even, dare I say, Carly. Her raspy voice, her peasanty looks—she seemed so down to earth, so heartfelt. She was definitely a "Natural Woman." As a review of the concert I read in the *Los Angeles Times* put it, "she is very capable of transmitting a chill with the clarity and honesty of her songs." My chillometer was on high.

Four months later Carole released *Tapestry;* an immediate hit, it shot to number one on the charts and stayed there for fifteen weeks. In May she returned to the Troubadour as the headliner, and Greg and I went to see her seven times. Replacing Molly as my sidekick,

Greg joined me as we tried to sneak up to Carole's dressing room, but there were always men guarding her door.

That wasn't about to stop me.

The Tuesday after Sunday's closing night show, we were sitting in Greg's kitchen eating the buttery, doughy balls dusted with powdered sugar that his grandmother always baked—since her last name was Sapperstein, we called them "Sappho cookies." That's when inspiration struck.

"Do you have two empty notebooks?" I asked, wiping the powdered sugar off my chin.

"I think so. Come on." Greg got up from the table and sashayed toward his faux knotty-pine bedroom. He found two empty binders that lay on a shelf in a dusty pile next to the complete set of Anaïs Nin's diaries. We each cut out a picture of Carole from a music magazine and glued it to the cover of our binders.

"What are we doing?" he asked, rubbing the extra glue off the edges of his picture into little balls.

"THE KING CASE," I declared. "Only we can't write that on the cover. Our covert operation could be exposed. We have till the end of summer to accomplish our mission."

"Uhh . . . Just what *is* our mission?" Greg asked.

"We find Carole King and become friends with her."

THE KING CASE

Tuesday, May 25, 1971, 5:00 p.m. PST–Sunday, June 13

The last few weeks before summer vacation!! YIPPEE!! Greg and I have been doing research on Carole at the library and newsstands (writing down info from music mags). Too bad I can't get school credit—I'm working way harder on this than any homework I've ever done!! HA! We've found out that Carole King was born Carole Klein, in Brooklyn, and she wrote some of the '60s greatest hits with her husband (#1), Gerry Goffin. I've compiled a complete discography of every song she's ever written (in a separate notebook—too long to put in here). I also wrote letters to her old record labels, using a fake name. Example:

> To Whom It May Concern:
>
> *My name is Madelyn Evans, and I'm a reporter for the L.A.–based music magazine,* Beat City. *I am writing an article on Carole King and it would be incredibly helpful if I could make mention of her out-of-print albums. If you'd be so kind as to send me one for the purpose of research, I'd greatly appreciate it.*
>
> Sincerely, Madelyn Evans

Beat City! *Isn't that a good one?!? It worked!!!!! I was sent a rare album from 1964 called* Dimension Dolls *(or as Greg says, "Dimension Dollllllllls")!!!!!!! I'm also pasting in some photos I found of Carole and her NEW husband (#2), Charlie Larkey—he plays with the band Jo Mama (I LOVE Abigale Haness, the lead singer!!!!) (But not as much as Carole!). The pics are with their kids, at home. So maybe we can use them as reference to help find their house. Some clues:*

wood fence

stairs could be in front or back

white stucco wall

notice light switch

the whole family "up on the roof" (tee hee)

weird squiggly pattern on gray

I'm also pasting in a MAP OF LAUREL ~~CNAYON~~ *CANYON, where everybody lives. I read an article in* Rolling Stone *that says Laurel Canyon is populated by the crème de la crème of Woodstock Nation's aristocracy. Not only Carole lives there but Carly, Joni, James, Frank Zappa, Crosby, Stills & Nash, and I think two Mamas and one Papa. If that's not crème de la crème, I don't know what is!!!*

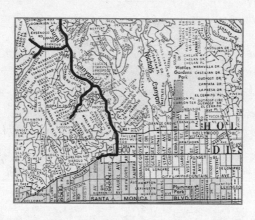

And guess what? The guys in Jo Mama are also Carole's backup band, YEP!! So I got all their addresses out of the phone book (too bad Carole's wasn't listed!!). The members are:

> *Ralph Schuckett*
> *Danny "Kootch" Kortchmar*
> *Abigale Haness (Did I mention I LOVE HER?!?)*
> *Joel O'Brien*

We're sure to get some clues from them.

Friday, June 18

DONE WITH SCHOOL! ADIOS JUNIOR HIGH!!! Greg and I spend the weekend marking up our maps and listening to Carole records. "So far away, doesn't anybody stay in one place anymore. It would be so fine to see your face at my door." Cool. Cuz, Carole, YOU'RE GONNA!!!!

Monday, June 21

This is REALLY the first day of THE KING CASE. The other days were just prep. So let's try that again. . . .

<u>DAY #1</u>

Monday, June 21

9:00 a.m. While all our friends go off to camp or are wasting their time at the beach, Greg and I head to Laurel Canyon. Mom's the only one we tell about THE CASE, since she's gonna drop us off and pick us up every day. YOU RULE, MOM!!! She says she's cool to take me anywhere as long as I don't end up like my brother—IN TROUBLE! HA! We drive out of Bel Air, cruise down Sunset Boulevard, through Westwood and Beverly Hills. At Doheny, the gi-normous rolling lawns stop as we hit the Sunset Strip. We pass Pat Collins the Hip Hypnotist's Celebrity Club (SHE'S SO FUNNY! She was on Lucy and made everyone act like washing machines!), then Gazarri's, then the Whisky a Go Go, and then we hit Laurel Canyon Boulevard, where we make a left, and then it feels like we're suddenly in the country. Not bandanas and wagon wheels—more like rolling papers and tie-dye!! I'm wearing cutoffs and a peasant blouse, and Greg's in his famous plaid grandpa shorts and one of his vintage gabardine shirts, all our clothes scored at the Goodwill for under a dollar (!) so we blend right in with the hippies here.

Mom drops us off "right smack dab in the middle" (a Carole lyric from "Up on the Roof"!) of the canyon at the Laurel Canyon Country Store. Our first in-depth investigation of the day is on Stanley Hills Drive, where Carole's keyboard player, Ralph Schuckett, lives.

I knock on his front door, and Ralph opens it!!! SIMPLE AS THAT! He's wearing jean shorts and a white T-shirt, looking way more casual than I've seen him in concert.

"Hi," I jump in. Greg isn't sure about what I'm up to yet, so he just stands there. "Sorry to bother you. We've been walking a long way from Sunset Bou-

levard and have a long way to go. Would it be possible to use your bathroom for a minute?"

"Sure, come on in," Ralph says.

Even though the Manson Family murders happened at Sharon Tate's house not that far from the canyon, Ralph is cool and trusting. Not that swishy Greg and fat-ass me look like murderers!!!! Tee hee.

I motion to Greg to use the bathroom first. I get a chill when I peek into the tiny living room and see Ralph's electric piano.

"So, are you a musician?" I ask, acting clueless.

"Yeah, I am."

"Cool. Do you play in a band?"

"Yeah, it's called Jo Mama." Ralph says it like he doesn't think I'll recognize the name. But he doesn't know who he's dealing with!!!!!

"No way?! I've seen you play! I saw you with James Taylor and Carole King." I say her name as if it's any old name, and I say it fast. "You guys are great!" I add.

"Thanks." He beams. "Hey, since you've still got a long way to go, would you like some cold lemonade?"

"Sure. Thanks."

By the time Greg walks out of the bathroom, Ralph is serving me lemonade and chatting up a storm. It's hysterical! On any other day, on any other "case," I might find sitting on a low couch covered in paisley material, talking it up with one of L.A.'s coolest keyboard players exciting, even memorable. But we're on a mission, and we have just the summer to complete it. The clock is a tickin', Ralphie baby!!!

Then Greg says, all brilliant, "Since you've played with Carole King it must be nice for you to see all the success she's having with Tapestry."

RIGHT ON! Greg's proving to be a worthy co-conspirator. I look expectantly at Ralph.

"Oh man, it's incredible," he answers. "One day she's sewing curtains for me, the next day she's a superstar."

He motions to the Indian print curtains hanging on four windows. I stare at them, speechless. Carole has touched that fabric, sewn them, stitch by stitch. Hell, she might have written "Tapestry" while making those very curtains. It makes sense, doesn't it???

"Ralph, could I have another glass of lemonade?" I am parched from the thrill of it all. But damn, Ralph doesn't give us any other clues. Instead, we drink so much lemonade that by the time we move on to Carole's guitarist Danny Kootch's house and launch into the "could we use your bathroom" ploy, I REALLY DO HAVE TO PEE!!

DAY #4

Thursday, June 24

I know I haven't written in here for a bit but even though we spend every day in Laurel Canyon, there really hasn't been anything much to report. More soon. SWEAR.

DAY #15

Monday, July 5

We lost a few days cuz of Fourth of July weekend. But for the past few weeks Greg and I have used similar ruses to get into the rest of Carole's band members' houses. We've seen a ton of paisley-material-covered couches (popular!), heard a ton of stories about the music scene in L.A., and drunk ten tons of lemonade—both pink and yellow. We even found Frank Zappa's house and also met Joni Mitchell's maid!!!!! (Remember it was Carole's babysitter who became Little Eva and had a hit with Carole's song "The Locomotion." Ya never know if Joni's maid will become a star, too!)

But it's Day #15 and we're no closer to meeting Carole in person than we were at the start. And I'm beginning to totally bum out.

Greg and I are having our usual breakfast this morning—Almond Joy bars and barbecue potato chips—in the parking lot of the Country Store, when I break the news. "I think we should just forget about THE KING CASE."

"Dollllllll, what else do we have to do this summer?"

Hillary Carlip

"More than just wandering aimlessly around Laurel Canyon. I just can't do this any more without making any progress." I put the bag of potato chips to my mouth and shake it, catching the last of the barbecue crumbs. "I'm gonna go get a Dr Pepper. Want one?"

"Why not."

And there, just as I'm about to call it quits, throw in the towel, say "Adios, Amigo," Fate steps into the tiny, four-aisle store. There he is, right in the frozen food section picking out TV Dinners (who knew Fate ate TV Dinners?!!) It's Charlie Larkey, Carole's husband (#2)!!!!!!!!!!!!!!!!

I pretend to examine some granola while keeping an eye on him. When he's at the checkout counter, I nonchalantly walk back outside.

"Come on!" I grab Greg just as Charlie strolls out, carrying his groceries. As he puts them in the backseat of his dark blue VW Bug, I walk up to him.

"Excuse me—are you going up the canyon? Can we hitch a ride?"

"Sure, hop in."

I hold the front seat up so Greg can climb in back, then I sit next to Charlie. He's way more handsome in person than in his pictures. I can see what Carole sees in him—even if he does sort of have a big beak. I tremble just knowing that Carole has actually ridden in this very car. Hell, she might have written "I Feel the Earth Move" in this car. It makes sense, doesn't it???

I need a glass of lemonade.

"Where are you guys going?" Charlie asks.

Since he's heading north, I take my chances. "Up Lookout."

"So am I," he says. I slip my hand into the backseat and squeeze Greg's leg. "Cool," I reply ever so casually.

"Where up Lookout?"

Shit. "Uh . . . well . . . um. . . . " I stammer.

"We're early meeting some friends, so we were just gonna walk around up there to kill some time," Greg chimes in. "Wherever you're going is cool. We'll walk from there."

I could kiss Greg's feet, except he's wearing his $13.00 sandals from Tijuana and his feet are totally gross—all sweaty and dirty.

When Charlie turns up Wonderland, I am so tempted to confess our un-

dying devotion and adoration for his wife and then ask questions that only he can answer: "What does she eat for breakfast?" "What time of the day does she write songs?" "Do her eyes close when she's laughing?" But I keep my cool.

Charlie pulls up to a curb and parks on the street in front of a house that's hidden by tall, thick bushes. The air smells like Froot Loops, all sweet and sugary, pink and purple. I see a For Sale sign hanging on a white post over the curb.

"This is as far as I'm going," Charlie says as he jostles the gears so the car won't roll down the steep hill. We jump out and say, maybe a little too enthusiastically, "Thank you soooooo much for the ride!"

"Sure. No problem."

He disappears behind the tall, bushy bushes and we wait anxiously, hoping to hear his wife greet him at the door. But we don't hear anything. DAMN! When we're sure the coast is clear, we jump up and down and hug each other—not in a spin-the-bottle, seven-minutes-in-heaven kind of a way, but more like Maxwell Smart and Agent 99.

"Can you believe it?" I squeal.

"Damn right," Greg cries. He swaggers over to the mailbox and peeks inside while I stand guard.

"Check this out." He hands me an envelope addressed to Carole Larkey. My heart stops. I sort through some more mail until I come across something shiny.

"Pay dirt." I show Greg a letter from the Department of Motor Vehicles. You know how they send those key chains with a mini version of your license plate? Well, that small black-and-yellow plate is shining through the envelope's clear plastic window, callin' out to us.

I know this isn't for Charlie's car. Any competent spy would have recorded his license plate in her case book the second she got out of his car (812 BRD).

This license plate key chain has to be for Carole: 545 APC.

We're in business. Now we'll just wait until we see her car parked in front of the house or in the driveway.

We sit quietly for about an hour. The only sounds are from three cawing crows circling above and the loud tick of my wristwatch—the one with the caricature of "Tricky Dick" Nixon (BOO, HISS!) that I picked out when I was

Hillary Carlip

visiting Nanny in Columbus, Ohio, and she took me to Lazarus department store and let me pick out any one thing.

"Shit, it's already four fifty-five," I shriek.

We tear ass outta there, flying down Wonderland Avenue, turning onto Lookout, and running down Laurel Canyon, the momentousness of our day's accomplishment carrying us down the hill in record time.

Mom's waiting in the parking lot of the store. "Any luck?" she asks like she always does when she picks us up. With all the mystery books she reads, I think Mom has a covert detective streak and is living vicariously through THE KING CASE.

"Yes, today we had a lot of luck," I proudly state.

DAY #16

Tuesday, July 6

Bright and early this morning, we return to the house on Wonderland. All day we wait for Carole, for 545 APC.

DAY #17

Wednesday, July 7

We return the next day . . .

DAY #18–DAY #25

Thursday, July 8–Thursday, July 15

. . . and the next, for a whole week. A few people traipse in and out of the house, but Carole is nowhere in sight. In the afternoon, we're sitting on the curb across from the house when Greg announces, "You were right. This is a bust. Let's just forget about it and go to the beach."

"What? But we're so close! Maybe she's just out on tour or something."

"In her car?" Greg slumps down and leans back against some neon purple bougainvillea.

"You can't give up now," I beg.

"Why not? You almost did last week."

"Yeah, but then we got a break. We're at her house now, aren't we?"

"Yeah, but she's not."

"Just give me one more day. I'll get another break in the case, I promise."

"How?"

"I don't know. . . . One more day."

"All right." Greg sighs.

<u>DAY #26</u>

Friday, July 16

Early this morning I ask Mom to take me to the library next to the car wash on San Vicente. I have an idea. If it doesn't work, THE KING CASE could be over and done with TODAY!

At 8:45 a.m., MY IDEA PAYS OFF!!!!!!!! I find a two-year-old phone book with Carole Larkey's address (on Wonderland) and . . . TA DA! Her phone number!!!! When we pick up Greg, I proudly flap the number in front of him.

"So?" Greg isn't at all excited.

"DUH!! We go do something else and just keep calling her. When she answers, we'll know she's there, and then we'll hurry up to her house," I say confidently.

The only fool in my foolproof plan is me! I haven't discussed any of this with anyone else, namely our chauffeur.

"Whoa, Hill, I have a lot of things to do," my mom says, pulling over to the curb. "I'll drop you off anywhere you want and pick you up, but, sorry, I can't drive you kids around all day."

SHIT! I sit in painful silence, looking at my partner in crime, who's about to bail. The trying-to-convince tactic hasn't worked at all, so I switch gears. I say softly, using big, sad, Keane-painting eyes, "Can we just give it a few more days? Plllleeeeeeaase?"

My Keane eyes win.

So for the zillionth time we hike up the hill to Carole's house on Wonder-

Hillary Carlip

land. And as if I had gotten on my knees and prayed for a break, for the first time in weeks there is actually some activity at the house!!!! A nicely dressed middle-aged couple is leaving. And just as they drive away, a car slows down, pulls over, and parks in front. A man with big, frizzy hair (not as big as my brother Howard's hair!!) steps out, then disappears behind Carole's bushes. We hear the front door open and close.

"What do you think is going on?" I whisper.

Greg shrugs, disinterested. "Not a clue."

And then suddenly, it all makes sense: why Carole hasn't been around. Why we never see 545 APC or 812 BRD parked in front. It's a sign. Right there in front of our faces. Literally. It says Open House.

DUH!!!!!!!!!! I CAN'T BELIEVE WE'VE BEEN SO STUPID!!! We saw a For Sale sign there on Day #15 and never put it together. What kind of detectives are we? We should turn in our badges right here and now. We'll never be as good as Mannix, McCloud, McMillan, OR Wife!! Carole's probably already moved. We'll have to start all over, and I know Greg won't go for that. Shit. I pull myself together.

"Come on, let's go in. We'll pretend we're prospective buyers."

"What?" Greg looks at me like I'm cracked. "Like anyone's gonna believe that? We're fourteen!"

"You have any other bright ideas?" We're getting real testy with each other now. "At least we can see where she's been living. Will you just stop being so crabby and come in with me?"

"Me, crabby? What about you?"

I feel my bottom lip begin to curl just like my dad's. "Can we discuss this later?"

When we walk into the house, we see that it's empty; shimmering hardwood floors and pristine white walls are the only remnants of the previous owners. Crap.

"Hi, may I help you?" a perky, balding Realtor in a beige suit asks.

"Yes, we're interested in the house." I coyly loop my arm through my fake husband/boyfriend/roommate's arm. I know that Carole is pregnant and expecting her third child, so I take a gamble. "Except we're looking for something a bit bigger. We have a large family. Is that why the previous owners are selling?"

"Well, yes, I think so," the Realtor answers.

I continue probing. "Do you happen to know if the owners stayed in Laurel Canyon? Maybe we could look in the area where they moved?"

Greg rolls his eyes at me like I asked the lamest question in all the land.

"Yes, they did," the Realtor responds. "They moved to Appian Way."

HA!! SEE?! Boy, do I give Greg a look back. Then I say, "Thanks. Hey, could I get one of your cards, please?" I ask this for Greg's sake, hoping that going one step further with the fake-out will amuse him and snap him out of his crabbiness.

The Realtor fishes a business card out of his coat pocket and hands it to me, then Greg and I stroll out to the street.

"You in?" I ask Greg.

"What the hell. Let's check out Appian Way." Then he adds, "Boy, that Realtor sure was a jackass, telling us everything like he did."

"Either that or he was totally impressed by our balls."

We pull out a map from my army knapsack. Appian Way is only about five streets away. At least that's how it looks on a map where you don't see steep hills. But walking those five blocks takes us more than an hour. By the time we reach Carole's new street, I'm panting heavily.

Note: Rethink my diet of Sappho cookies, potato chips, and Dr Pepper!

"Now all we have to do," I say, gasping for breath, "is go up and down the street and look for 545 APC or 812 BRD." And we're off. . . .

DAY #29–DAY #40

Monday, July 19–Friday, July 30

We spend the next week and a half trudging up the canyon to Appian Way, looking for Carole and Charlie's cars. When we don't see them, I come up with Plan B to keep Greg interested. We begin to visit random houses, knocking on doors with fake excuses. "Sorry to bother you, but we're lost. Can you explain how to get back down to Wonderland?" "We're waiting for our friends, who aren't home yet, and we really have to use a bathroom. Would you mind?" "My mom ran out of gas. Could we use your phone?" Everyone is kind, and when they welcome us in, one of us goes into the bathroom or writes down directions or pretends to use the phone while the other looks around, searching for clues—a piano, family portraits, or a room that matches the pictures we've seen of Carole's house. But, CRAP, we find nothing.

Between the hour-long hike up the steep hills and the door-to-door scheming, by the end of the day we're exhausted. At the top of Appian Way we find a rest stop, a lookout point blanketed with orange trumpet flowers and stinky (good stinky) sage. There's a tree that has low branches for us to sit on and a killer view of the city. The stillness is so unfamiliar and, well, kinda unsettling. At home there's always noise: Howard banging on his drums; Mom and Dad's blaring television, which they fall asleep to every night; my records constantly playing.

One afternoon I clear my throat and say softly, "Sorry."

"For what?" Greg asks.

"For dragging you up here and ruining your summer vacation. It was a crazy idea."

"Well, yeah. . . . "

"Allright. Let's go. We're done." I take Greg's hand and pull him up from the ground. We're brushing the sage off our pants when we hear a voice. I SWEAR. Right when we're about to call it quits again. It's so spooky how that keeps happening! The voice is unmistakable. No one else in the whole wide world has that voice, which the Los Angeles Times called "raspy, tender-tough, rawly whining-pleading, pulsing: delightfully unpolished. Real."

IT'S CAROLE.

Saying good-bye to some friends at her door.

In the house . . .

. . . DIRECTLY ACROSS THE STREET FROM US!!!!!

Oh. My. GOD! ! ! ! ! ! ! ! ! ! ! ! ! ! ! !

We hear her front door close, and I grab Greg. "Come on."

Her friends—two men and a lady—are dressed all in white. As they climb into a tan VW van, I call out, "Hey," trying to sound as cool as possible. "Can we hitch a ride down the hill with you?"

"Sure," the taller of the two guys says.

We hop into the backseat with the lady. On the dashboard are several pictures of an old, mystical-looking Indian man with a gray beard. Greg and I listen closely to Carole's friends.

"She's just so nice," the driver says. (We knew that.)

"It's not often you meet someone like that in yoga class," the taller man adds. (Yoga?!) "And it's really cool that she agreed to give some of the proceeds of her concerts to Swami Satchidananda's work." (Swami? Naturally.)

"She's very special," the lady coos. (DUH!!!!!!)

The van pulls into the Country Store parking lot and drops us off. We jump out, shouting, "Thanks for the ride."

Greg and I are dizzy with excitement. As we wait for my mom, we clink our Dr Pepper cans together and toast our achievement.

DAY #43–DAY #47

Monday, August 2–Friday, August 6

For the last five days Greg and I have watched the house from our lookout point while we decide exactly what to do now that we've found Carole. And here at last, this morning we finally have an actual sighting!!! We hide behind the tree as Carole pulls her car—545 APC—out of the gated driveway. That's why we never saw the cars. She and Charlie park behind a gate! DUH!

Once she disappears down the hill, we run to the front door and knock. Her eleven-year-old daughter, Louise Goffin, answers. Long wavy hair and blue, blue eyes, she looks older than she does in the photos I've seen. But she looks a lot like her mom.

Greg launches into our ploy, "Sorry to bother you, but we're waiting for our friends who aren't home yet and really have to use the bathroom. Would you mind?"

"I guess it's okay." Louise opens the door.

While Greg's in the bathroom, I scope out the joint. And there it is, larger than life, in front of a stained-glass window in her rustic, cozy living room.

Hillary Carlip

Carole's piano. A grand piano. Dark black. Shiny. Dear God, Buddha, Mary—
Swami Satchidananda—I pray silently in gratitude to all the forces at my spiri-
tual buffet, THANK YOU!

THE DAY!!!!

DAY #50

Monday, August 9

X marks the spot, mission accomplished, case closed!!!

I wake before dawn and bake banana bread. It worked with Carly, why
wouldn't it work with Carole? Greg and I head into the canyon, and before we
can chicken out, go right up to Carole's door and knock. And as simple as that,
after fifty-plus days on THE KING CASE . . .

CAROLE ANSWERS!!!!

There I am, standing face-to-face with the most talented woman not just on
Earth, but in the whole entire universe.

"Hello," she says in that voice.

I manage to get out a shaky "Hi."

"We just want to tell you that we really love your music," Greg steps in. I
pull myself together enough to add, "You're a real inspiration."

"Well, thank you so much." She is as kind and lovely as I expected she
would be. Though we knew Carole was pregnant, we aren't prepared for how
much she's showing! She looks like she's about to pop any second, though of
course, as any good detectives know, she isn't due until December.

I hold out our loaf of bread wrapped in one of my mother's pink linen nap-
kins. "We baked this for you, in appreciation. It's banana bread."

"How wonderful." She smiles as she takes our gift, her hand brushing mine.
And then the heavens smile down on us. Carole King says, "Why don't you
come in?"

Everything we've been working for is finally paying off!! We step inside.

Carole's house is as colorful and warm as her most soulful ballads. We follow her into the tiled kitchen, where she serves us pink lemonade, and we chat for almost an hour. I tell her about how we discovered her before anyone else did, how I tracked down her Dimension Dolls album (well, I leave out that I had posed as a reviewer from a fake magazine to get the album! HA!). We play with her German shepherds, Lyka and Schwartz, while she keeps refilling our lemonade glasses.

Then she says, "I'd invite you to swim in our pool, but it's full of algae." God bless her for even considering the invitation! She's a true star, worthy of every minute of our devotion. But the capper comes when Carole King, THE NUMBER ONE SINGE, lies down, right there on her tiled kitchen floor, and performs what she calls her "Lamaze" breathing exercises!!! I SWEAR!!! IT'S AMAZING!!! She wouldn't do that in front of just anyone. Only friends.

When it's time to leave, I start to really bum out. Even though we're now officially friends with Carole, we can't keep coming back to her house, can we? This is the end of the road—the end of THE KING CASE. We say good-bye to Carole—she even hugs us—and I do everything I can to be strong and not cry.

We did it. We befriended Carole King. Wow.

Wednesday, August 11–Friday, August 13

So what happens after you hang out with Carole King? You have to tell all your friends about it, NATCH! And just in case they don't believe us, Greg and I devise a scheme. As Hayley Mills constantly repeats in one of my favorite movies, The Trouble with Angels, "What a scathingly brilliant idea!"

I'd recently found a bootleg album of Carole playing a live concert. We pick the exact spots on the record where she speaks to the audience. We call each friend, and when they answer the phone, I tell them we're CALLING FROM CAROLE'S HOUSE! Then Greg expertly puts the needle down on the record where Carole says from the stage: "I'd like to introduce you to a good friend of mine."

Hillary Carlip

"Oh—hold on," I whisper into the phone. "Carole wants us to meet someone. How do you do? Nice meeting you, too."

Then I call some more of our friends, and, when I cue him, Greg puts the needle down in another spot on the record where Carole asks for a glass of water. I reply, "Greg, you go get it for her—I'm on the phone."

HA! All our friends totally buy it! Well, it isn't that far from the truth. If not for that damn algae, WE'D HAVE GONE SWIMMING IN CAROLE'S POOL!

It's Friday the thirteenth (BEWARE!), and I'm now sitting on my roof, where I'm writing my closing thoughts in my KING CASE notebook. I'm home alone, and it's quiet, except for a Good Humor ice cream truck tinkling its music box jingle as it heads up my empty street. Summer's almost over and soon I'll be starting high school. And ya know what? I think it's time to grow up and get real.

Face it. I'm not friends with Carole King any more than I was friends with Carly Simon. I know that. It's been neat meeting these people, but why did I even want to be friends with them to begin with? It's cuz I admire WHAT THEY DO. They're so talented and creative.

So the question is, WHY DON'T I JUST DO THAT MYSELF??? Well, first of all, I don't really want to be famous. I couldn't take all that attention! Secondly, what would I do? My singing sucks!!! This was confirmed last month when I was rehearsing for a guitar class recital in front of Ava Atkins and her older brother. I sang Simon and Garfunkel's "The Dangling Conversation," and when I reached for the high notes on, "As we sit and drink our coffee . . ." they burst out laughing and continued uncontrollably until I stopped singing. At the recital I ended up playing an instrumental version of the song, just strumming a bunch of stupid chords. So singing is definitely out. And I know (thanks to cotillion) that dancing is out, too. I do love to write (as you can see by my windbaggy journal entries!! HA!!). Or maybe I could be an actress like my fave, Carrie Snodgress, who I discovered when she was a guest kidney failure patient on an episode of Medical Center months before she starred in Diary of a Mad Housewife. *Or maybe an artist like another fave, Joni Mitchell, who paints all her album covers.*

I don't know. . . . But hey—if I could find Carole King, meet her, and watch her do Lamaze exercises on her kitchen floor, there is no telling what else I can do. Right?

That ice cream truck's a-callin' me. Gotta go get a Dreamsicle. BYE!

Hillary Carlip

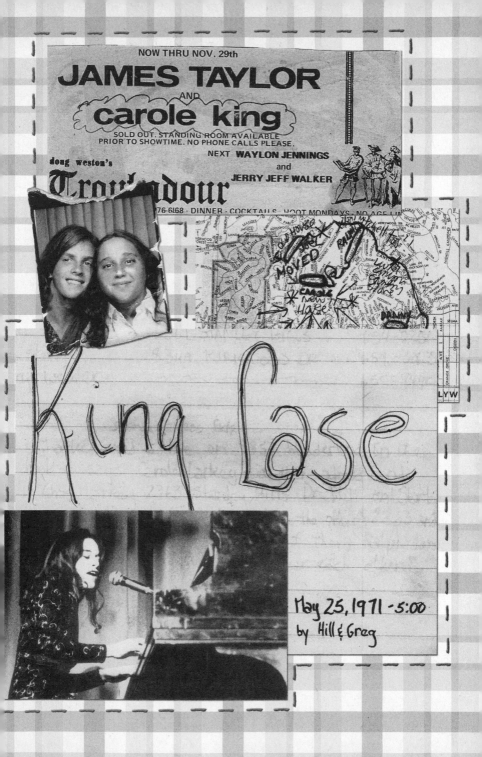

Spring
1972

✳ President Nixon makes an historic visit to China and brings back a pair of Chinese giant pandas: Hsing-Hsing and Ling-Ling.

✳ Shigei, a Japanese exchange student, moves into our house. For his art class assignment, he paints a still life of my brother's bong.

✳ For the first time ever, women are allowed to run in the Boston Marathon. I ditch P.E. almost every day.

✳ I scale Barbra Streisand's fence with my friend David. We leave a vase she admired at the antique store where David works, asking if she'd give us two tickets to the McGovern for President fundraiser where she's performing, since they cost $100.00 apiece. Two weeks later she actually sends us free tickets! Good thing we didn't mention the reason we want to go to the concert is to see Carole King and James Taylor, not her.

In Concert at the Forum-April 15th · 8:30 PM

Carole King   Barbra Streisand   James Taylor

McGovern
Use the Power ⅓ Register and Vote

Quincy Jones and his Orchestra

Ushers: Warren Beatty · Jack Nicholson · Julie Christie · Sally Kellerman · James Earl Jones · Jacqueline Bisset
Michelle Gilliam · Mike Nichols · Shirley MacLaine · Goldie Hawn · Gene Hackman · Elliott Gould
Marlo Thomas · Burt Lancaster · Jon Voight · Raquel Welch · Michael Sarrazin · Britt Ekland and more

✳ President Nixon indefinitely cancels the Paris Peace Talks. Six weeks later, he declares an escalation in the war, expanding the destruction against North Vietnam. I am a monitor at anti-war demonstrations, and protest alongside Jane Fonda while next to us pro-war groups carry signs and shout, "We're not fonda Fonda."

✳ The FAA announces all airlines must begin screening passengers and baggage before boarding due to increased terrorism worldwide.

✳ I see Shirley Chisholm, the first female African American presidential candidate, speak at the Santa Monica Civic Auditorium, and create a photo essay of the event for my high school photography class final. Shirley loses. I get a C.

Teen Libber

I was thirteen years old when women started burning their bras. Since I had just begun wearing one and was pretty damn excited about it, I opted out. But it was at that time I became what the *Los Angeles Times* two years later dubbed me: a "Teen Libber."

I had taken my first political stand at age nine by boycotting Sugar Daddies, Sugar Babies, and Junior Mints because the candy company that made them was run by the founder of the John Birch Society, a group of right-wing, anti-Semitic racists.

At first my boycott wasn't by choice—my mom and dad forbade my brother and me to buy the offending items. But I quickly felt the heady sense of empowerment that comes with taking action to fight injustice. Little did my parents know the impact this childhood boycott would have on my brother and me. By the time we hit high school we were both teenage activists.

In my freshman year (or, as I called it, "fresh*woman*" year) some friends and I started a women's consciousness-raising group. Fifteen of us met weekly, gathering in basements and bedrooms to discuss sexism, racism, classism, ageism, and any other -*ism* we could think of.

We weren't just talkers. We also took action. We prowled newsstands in Westwood Village and Santa Monica, plastering "This exploits women" stickers on *Glamour* and *Playboy* magazines. We produced the first-ever High School Women's Conference, where girls from all over Los Angeles gathered for workshops on Self-Defense and "High School Oppression," and participated in discussions on such hot topics as "Rock Culture and Chauvinism," whatever *that* was. At NBC Studios in Burbank we spearheaded a demonstration against Sexism in the Media, picketing the *Dean Martin Show* and his scantily clad Golddiggers. That landed us on the six o'clock news. Articles about us appeared in the *Evening Outlook* and the *Los Angeles Times*, headlines proclaiming: "High School Feminists Speak Out" and "Teen Libbers Fight for Own Cause." We were committed to a revolution.

But it was our weekly consciousness-raising sessions that had the biggest impact on me. And it was one particular meeting in the spring of 1972 that stands out most.

It was the night we gathered at Jill's house in Beverly Hills, just down the street from Zsa Zsa Gabor's gated estate. We sat in a circle on the living room floor alongside Jill's parents' collections of African fertility goddess statues and brightly woven textiles.

"We're gonna do something a little different," Jill, that night's leader, said, gathering her frizzy hair into a bun. Her unshaven armpits peeked out of her tank top. We were proud of *all* our hair.

"I want everyone to take off their clothes," she announced.

Murmurs of laughter spread as the group looked nervously at one another.

"Don't worry, my parents and brother are gonna be out late." And with a playful smile, Jill pulled her shirt over her head, revealing her small, perky breasts.

We laughed again; some of us even looked away. But we were determined to take risks and to support our "sisters" in those risks. So, once the initial awkwardness passed, one girl began to take off her clothes. Then another, and another. Shirts, then bras, pants, then underpants. Everyone was pumped. Everyone, that is, except me. I sat motionless and fully clothed.

"Hillary, you gonna join us?" Jill asked.

"Sure," I said as I slowly unbuckled one brown sandal. I was twenty-five pounds overweight, and letting a whole group witness all that flesh in the flesh was not my idea of fun. Yet to not participate would be even worse. I'd still be fat, *and* I'd be a loser.

I took a deep breath and gradually untied my embroidered peasant blouse. Another inhale and I slid out of my jeans. The others were already naked, watching me, so, my face turning red hot, I swiftly removed my bra and underwear and crossed my arms over my body, hunkering down into the rug.

Our circle of naked girls sat surrounded by the sculptures of African women with pendulous breasts as if we were participating in some tribal initiation. Jill nodded at us in approval. "The patriarch and the media teach us to hate our bodies. Women don't look like the bone-thin models in ads and commercials. We refuse to buy into the bullshit," she pronounced.

"Right on!" Cathy shouted, raising her fist in the air, revealing *her* hairy armpit.

"It's bullshit!" several others chimed in.

"So tonight," Jill continued, "we're gonna get into the middle of the circle, one at a time, and share at least three things we love about our bodies."

"Wow!" "Cool!" "Far out!" Everyone was keyed up. I was mortified.

Just one year earlier my parents had taken me to Weight Watchers. Only five feet tall, I shed 22 of my 140 pounds in three months, and the program awarded me a diamond achievement pin. But one week later I returned to my life of Sara Lee banana cake, Pepperidge Farm coconut cake, and Scooter Pies, and I gained back every pound, plus extra. My weight, I told myself, was a political statement—fat was a feminist issue. I was proving that I could love my body no matter its shape or size. I ate what I wanted to, when I wanted to, and I was proud of it. Or at least I thought I was. Until that night.

One by one, my naked friends stepped into the middle of the circle and sat.

Ava was first. I couldn't help but notice her shapely, large breasts. Her stomach was flat and tight, and she was blessed with the kind of curvy perfection that could have landed her on the pages of one of those offending magazines we plastered with stickers.

"I really love my calves. They're muscular and strong," she began. "I love my thighs, my waist, and my belly."

Who the hell loves her belly? I fidgeted, the nubs of the hand-woven African rug poking into my bare ass.

Ava smiled and returned to the circle as Molly, tall, blond, and striking, bounded into the middle and sat.

"I love my eyes and my nose. My stomach's cool, so are my legs. Actually, though, I hate my butt. It's—"

Jill interrupted. "We're only talking about what we love tonight. No judgments."

"Oh, well, then that's it."

To my relief Sarah was next. She was even more overweight than I was and extremely hairy. Everywhere. Surely she would have a hard time finding things she loved about her body.

I eagerly sat forward, but Sarah grinned. "I love the rolls on my stomach, my big womanly thighs, and my childbearing hips. But mostly, I love my hairy chest."

I felt nauseous and light-headed.

I was next in the circle. I rose slowly and shuffled into the middle. I sat with my knees up and my arms crossed, hiding as much of my perspiring body as I could.

"Well," I began, my voice shaking, "I like my teeth. You know what, I *love* my teeth." My head down, I stared at the rug so I didn't have to meet anyone's gaze. Instead I saw my unshaven legs with wiry dark hairs swirling across pale skin, my flabby stomach, and a bright red pimple on the inside of my fat left thigh.

I had to come up with something else, and fast.

"Um, oh, my hands are great. They're strong and dexterous. Uh . . . then . . . let's see. . . . " I stammered, "Well . . . you know, uh. . . ."

Hillary Carlip

I couldn't think of one other thing.

Suddenly I felt a tear dripping out of the eye I couldn't even say I loved, onto the cheek that hadn't made the list, either. There I sat, in the middle of the circle, naked and weeping.

I couldn't lie. "I hate my body."

Hot with shame, I slowly stood up to return to my place. But then, without a word, fourteen naked girls rose and encircled me.

"I love your thighs," Molly said softly. "They're perfectly proportioned and strong as hell."

"I love your stomach," Ava called out. "It's soft and inviting."

"I love it, too," Sarah and Diane agreed.

"Your breasts are incredible. So big and round and full," Jill said.

This went on and on, my friends heaping praise and compliments—whether they were true or not—on my unloved body: "You have deep, soulful eyes," "A perfect nose," "Your feet are so petite and cute."

I cried harder. Not only was I moved by the generosity of my sisters, but I also realized that here I was, in a relationship with my body *for life,* and I hadn't once cared for it. It was like being stuck in a loveless marriage.

In that moment, in that room, surrounded by love and support, for the first time ever, I actually felt ... well ... sort of beautiful. I decided right then and there that I would commit the feeling to memory like an actress learning her lines until the character becomes totally natural. Through my weight's ups and downs, through being thick or thin, I would hold on to my fellow Teen Libbers' kind words and start the revolution within.

ROBIN PRENTISS
...breed of oppression.

HILLARY CARLIP
...taking consequences.

ANNIE GOLDBERG
...no identity of own

DORI SCHACK
...easier to change.

RUTHY GRAF
...first step taken

Teen Libbers Fight for Own Cause

BY BARBARA RIKER
West Side Women's News Editor

Teen-age women's liberationists on the West Side have formed a consciousness raising group to combat what they call the "high school breed of oppression against women."

They meet weekly to discuss how to change stereotypes which affect them as high school women.

The teen-agers feel that although they are young, they have already been molded by sexual stereotypes, and they say it is hard to change.

"I suppose it is easier for us than for our mothers to change, but even so we have already had 15 years of thinking of ourselves in the old ways," said Dori Schack, 17.

First Step

"Don't get the impression that we are all liberated," said Ruthy Graf, 17. "We have taken the first step because we have started questioning the old attitudes.

"But it is so hard not to play games like acting dumb to get a boyfriend, or being jealous of somebody else's date."

"There is a whole high school breed of oppression against women," said Annie Goldberg, 16. "You don't have an identity of your own, but are rated on whom you are dating."

Stereotyped Roles

Robin Prentiss, 17, said that high school girls are stereotyped in their roles academically as well as socially.

"There is a sexual tracking system in high schools," she said. "The women are supposed to take typing and the men take drafting or shop.

"They never even hint that high school women should learn a skill, and this leads to an enormous unskilled labor market. Untrained women get bad jobs for bad pay.

"I know this is a problem because I am out of high school and I can't find a job."

The young women agreed that in middle-class families girls are expected themselves to rather than ea

"People granted that y ry and be m your husband said. "The they think should be ei that her hus joy talking w

The teen said that wh their parents their particip women's mov are accepting.

"My mother the moveme says she feels quences of g accepted pat Hillary Carlip

Members c sciousness r held a women in the spring work for birt abortion coun high schools Most of them versity High

They discus issues relatin and say they ed in more th for equal wo

"I couldn't am equal to I think bein America is n of an ideal t Miss Graf sa just as trapp types as we a

"What I p just to be ab

EVENING OUTLOOK   Mon., March 27, 1972

Laurie   Hillary

High School Feminists

Continued From Page 10
and writing about. I asked if I could do one on abortion. She said, 'No, you can't, that's not a fit topic for mixed company.'

"Then once I signed up for auto shop. I was saving money to get a car and I wanted to know how it worked. That's a perfectly legitimate thing to want to know about — how to take care of your car.

"The counselor said I would have to ask the autoshop teacher. So I did. The first thing he said was that I would get my clothes dirty. I said I would bring overalls. Then he started with the 'There's only one bathroom in the building'

bathroom before or after class, and I lifted the brake unit. Then he got mad and said he just didn't want girls in his class."

Molly, whose main interest is art said she had taken a horticulture class. "The teacher has changed his attitudes now, but he first semester, he would say things like 'Okay, you men go work in the plots. Girls, you can go pick up loose cement."

The women said they all get good grades, Stephanie commented. "We work hard with the books and we like our classes. But a lot of times it seems like the teachers and counselors (most are women) bim

"Counselors," Molly added, "will say 'you could be such a good student' if you would dress a certain way or if you weren't political. And these kinds of attitudes not only oppress women students, but the men as well. That's why liberation is important."

How has feminism affected their lives? "I used to believe in evolution rather than revolution," said Stephanie, who would like to become a math teacher.

"I thought that maybe in 20 or 30 years things would change. But I don't feel that way anymore. That kind of attitude is like buck-passing, because

Summer 1972

* I work day and night at the McGovern for President headquarters. He wins the Democratic nomination! Two weeks later my co-volunteers and I are all depressed when McGovern drops his running mate, Thomas Eagleton, after it's revealed he had electroshock therapy to treat depression.

* See Ingmar Bergman's *Cries and Whispers* four times. I am fixated with the scene where the young maid cradles a woman against her bare breast. Develop huge crush on Liv Ullmann.

* See *Anne of the Thousand Days* three times. Develop huge crush on Genevieve Bujold.

* Develop huge crush on my best friend, Karen.

* Since I'm so conflicted about my sexuality, the number one song on the *Billboard* charts sums up my existence: "Alone Again (Naturally)."

✳ Five men are arrested breaking into the Democratic headquarters at the Watergate Hotel.

✳ As my high school women's consciousness-raising group continues to meet weekly, the first issue of *Ms.* magazine is published. It's an immediate success—all 300,000 copies sell in eight days.

✳ The musical *Hair* ends its Broadway run after 1,742 performances. I see it when it plays in L.A. at the Aquarius Theatre and almost miss the most infamous part, as I desperately have to pee and am heading to the ladies room. Luckily, I catch the nude scene from the back of the theater.

✳ A week after Nixon and Agnew are nominated for re-election by the Republican National Convention, Nixon claims at a press conference that an investigation of the Watergate break-in, led by White House counsel John Dean, has revealed that no one employed by the administration had anything to do with the bugging.

(Heart) Breaking News

The day my seventeen-year-old brother led the police on a high-speed chase in my parents' Lincoln Continental and ended up going to a mental hospital, I went to Grauman's Chinese Theatre and saw *Fantasia*.

That summer my mother volunteered, transcribing books for the blind. She toiled daily on a Braille typewriter, transforming the novel *The World of Suzie Wong* into tiny raised dots. My dad spent his weekends wearing paint-splattered shirts and espadrilles, carving ancient Egyptian scenarios into wooden shutters for the den. I was fifteen and going through my Zen period; I meditated, chose a Zen name (Munan Duvi) and read *Zen Flesh, Zen Bones* until the pages were worn. And Howard, the only white boy in upscale Bel Air to sport a huge afro, fell under the spell of Carlos Castaneda's Don Juan books and decided to experiment with hallucinatory drugs.

Howard was a high school revolutionary. One of the founders of a notorious underground school newspaper called the *Red Tide*, he wrote scathing anti-establishment articles and organized countless demonstrations at school. Carrying the flag of the United Farm Workers and passing out flyers, he urged students to boycott the cafeteria until the school stopped serving grapes; he picketed outside Auto Shop, demanding that girls be allowed to take the boys-only class, and he staged an anti-war protest in the administration building—a gathering so large, the school had to shut down for the day. Howard was out to make the world a better place and, despite our brother-sister bickering, he was my hero.

With my newfound Eastern philosophy, courtesy of the books I purchased at the Bodhi Tree Bookstore in West Hollywood, I tried to stay in the moment at all times, tried to remain nonjudgmental and accept "what is." But while I was sleeping with *Music for Zen Meditation* playing softly on my turntable, my brother was eating peyote buttons and sleeping in the lilac bushes on the hill in back of our suburban home.

My mother and I began noticing something was really off with Howard when one day the three of us were climbing into the Lincoln Continental to go to the supermarket. I automatically opened the back door since my older brother always had "dibs on shotgun." Only on this day, with the early summer Santa Ana winds stirring up trouble, Howard darted into the backseat, practically knocking me down.

"Sit in the front," he commanded.

"Really? What's the occasion?"

"Just do it."

I didn't argue. I jumped in front. As we took off, my brother slid across the backseat until he was lying flat, his large afro squished against the passenger door.

"Turn left, they're following us!" he suddenly shouted.

"Who?" my mom asked as she looked in the rearview mirror and saw no one.

"The same guys who are tapping our phone. *Turn left now!*"

My mother did turn left, but then she pulled over to the curb. "How, what's going on?"

I chimed in. "Look, there's no one even behind us."

"Trust me, they're there. They must have ducked out of sight. They're very shrewd."

Okay. My seventeen-year-old brother was together enough to

say someone was "very shrewd," but he was hiding in the backseat, blathering in bizarre paranoia.

"And just who do you think is tapping our phone?" my mother probed.

"I don't *think* they are—I *know* they are. They're after me."

"Who?" she persisted.

"The FBI. Just drive. *Drive!*"

Frightened, my mother flipped on her turn signal and pulled back into the traffic. She just looked at me and remained silent while Howard shouted out directions.

"Faster. *Faster!*"

"Turn right."

"Pull in front of that car. Quick!"

Now, my brother's saying that the FBI was tapping our phones and following him wasn't that much of a stretch, given his political activities. But even if it were true, there were probably more rational ways of dealing with the situation than lying down in the backseat of the car shouting out directions to nowhere.

We drove around for fifteen minutes more, until my mother gathered her courage and declared, "Forget groceries, we're going home."

When we reached the house, Howard ran upstairs to his room. I loved his room. I'd often sneak in there to look at the psychedelic Day-Glo posters of Jimi Hendrix and John Lennon that plastered the walls alongside the "Free Angela" and "Free Huey" bumper stickers stuck on his closet door, all eerily illuminated by a black light.

I followed my mother into the kitchen and sat at the white Formica table as she made herself a martini and pulled a bottle of pills out of the cupboard. She took a gulp of her cocktail, washing down a Miltown.

"What are you gonna do?" I asked.

Trying not to cry, she paced back and forth on the gold-speckled linoleum. My mom's frosted hair, which she had just gotten done at the beauty parlor the day before, was wilting in the heat, despite the stiff spray holding it together like a helmet.

"I'm going to wait until your father gets home."

She took another swig of her martini, ate the green olive floating on top, tossed the pit in the trash, then began to yank vegetables out of the refrigerator and throw them into a large pot on the stove. She cut up an onion and allowed its bitter sting to finally release her tears. When my father arrived a half hour later, my mother intercepted him at the door.

"Would you go talk to your son? He's really freaking out," she said, compulsively wiping her hands on her "Kiss the Chef" apron. As she explained what had happened earlier, my father just shook his head. He stamped his cigarette out in one of the large glass ashtrays that sat everywhere around the house, took another Benson and Hedges out of the pack in his shirt pocket, and lit it with a book of matches from Scandia. "It's drugs, isn't it?" he stated more than asked, deeply inhaling his frustration and keeping it locked in his lungs. He then trudged up the stairs.

My mother called out, "After you talk, bring him down for dinner. Tell him we're having beef stew."

My father knocked on my brother's door and disappeared into the black-lit room. Twenty minutes later he led Howard downstairs, and we all sat at the kitchen table and ate dinner like any normal family. I looked at my brother and squeezed potatoes through the spaces between my teeth, which always made him laugh. When he didn't even crack a smile, I knew something was wrong. Terribly wrong.

Over the next week or two, Howard grew more distressed and defiantly refused to listen to any parental reasoning. Finally my mother said, "We've made an appointment for you to see someone. We're getting you help."

My brother shouted back indignantly, "Don't you see *that's* who's after me?"

"Who?"

Hillary Carlip

"*Them,*" he answered cryptically.

"No one's after you," my father said gently yet firmly. "We're talking about a counselor who can help you deal with the situation."

"There's nothing wrong with me," my brother shouted even louder, then slammed the door and stomped out to the bushes to take a nap.

A week later, it was Howard's graduation night from University High School. A few months prior, he had been expelled from Uni for trying to sell an issue of the *Red Tide* for ten cents to his social studies teacher. The principal defended the expulsion by explaining that selling *anything* on campus was illegal. Even though the writers of the newspaper used pseudonyms, the administration knew who was behind the *Red Tide*, and they were looking for any excuse to suspend or expel the perpetrators. Howard became the first sacrificial lamb.

My brother had transferred to Hamilton High for the remaining months of his senior year. When he was invited to graduate with his old class at Uni and once again play drums with the school band, he was thrilled. I wasn't sure why since he hated the school that had expelled him, and was by no means finished with the political activities that got him kicked out in the first place. When I asked him why he was going to the graduation, he ominously replied, "You'll find out soon enough."

Since the auditorium at Uni High was too small for the large senior class, graduation was held in Pauley Pavilion, a cavernous hall at UCLA. I sat with my mother and father, and we searched the crowded stage, finding Howard, in his cap and gown, playing with the band. My parents smiled proudly, relieved that this chapter in my brother's life was finally coming to an end. The ceremony was uneventful until the principal called Howard up to receive his diploma.

My brother stood, ripped off his graduation gown, and exposed a T-shirt that was emblazoned, front and back, in bright red, revolutionary lettering: FUCK HIGH SCHOOL.

He ran around the stage to make sure everyone could see it, then tore-ass out of the auditorium to resounding cheers. Moments later the fire alarm sounded, forcing everyone to evacuate the building in the middle of the ceremony. To this day no one knows for sure if my brother, in one last authority-riling crescendo, set off that alarm or not, though the timing was uncanny.

At home later that night, Howard seemed calmer. In fact, he seemed so together the next day, my parents left for Palm Springs as they had earlier planned.

Twenty-four hours later, on a quiet Sunday morning, the police spotted a suspicious-looking, freaky, seventeen-year-old white boy with lilac leaves and twigs knotted into his afro, driving a fancy car in an upscale neighborhood at 6:00 a.m. They tried to pull him over for questioning, but Howard took off.

The high-speed police pursuit started in Bel Air, continued east on Sunset Boulevard, then swerved north into a posh gated community where Howard and the police sped through twisting, narrow streets lined with estates.

If this had occurred today, the chase would interrupt television programming; it would be shown live from various choppers. *Breaking news.* A graphic and a snappy title would accompany the story: "Bel Air 'Burb Boy Provokes Police Pursuit." While reporters added drama, we'd hear:

"It looks like a light-skinned African American male."

"He possibly stole the car."

"He may have a gun."

But back then the only ones who ever knew the pursuit occurred were the few early-morning onlookers collecting their newspapers from their driveways—and my grandparents, who were called to bail Howard out of jail after he was arrested when, twenty minutes into the chase, he took a right turn and hit a dead-end street.

When my grandfather finally called my parents to give them the news later that afternoon, they rushed back from Palm Springs to find their teenage fugitive sitting at my grandparents' kitchen table eating a turkey sandwich and playing gin with my grandmother.

Meanwhile I was home alone reading a book of Zen quotes when a heavy rain shook me out of my contemplation. I listened to the thunder, loud and soft, and ran out to the backyard to greet the summer storm. Face up to dripping clouds, I smelled the downpour in my hair, licked it from my lips. I was a nature freak—I had made mobiles from driftwood and shells that I gathered at the beach, took hikes through the neighborhood hillsides, and picked flowers then dried them by tying the bouquets at the stem and hanging them upside down from a string I had tied across my bedroom.

I returned to my lavender bedroom, leaving the rain-slapped window wide open. I picked up my book again and started reading more Zen quotes. I was feeling calm and centered when the doorbell rang.

I opened the door to see Dr. Levenson, a close friend of my parents who was also our family physician.

"Hey, how ya doing?" I asked casually.

"Okay." His face looked unusually stern, void of emotion.

"Uh . . . my parents are out of town, and I'm the only one home."

"I know. They asked me to meet them here."

This did not sound good. Were they going to break the news that my mom had cancer or my dad had a brain tumor? "Is everything all right?"

"Well, no it's not."

I felt my knees start to weaken.

"Your brother's been arrested, and I'm here to do an intervention."

"A what?"

"He's on drugs. We're going to take him to a mental hospital."

"Oh. Wow."

The rain stopped, leaving one of those spectacular pink-and-orange L.A. sunsets in its wake. As Dr. Levenson filled me in on the news of my brother's attempt to flee from the police and his arrest, my parents drove up in the Lincoln Continental with Howard in the backseat. He jumped out of the car before it came to a stop and ran to his own dirty yellow Dodge Dart parked in the driveway in front of Dr. Levenson's shiny green Buick Electra.

Howard was so focused on getting out, he put the Dart into reverse and stepped on the gas. Tapping the doctor's Buick, he pulled forward, turned his steering wheel, and backed out again, trying to maneuver his way past the car. Again and again he hit the gas, turned the wheel, the tires rubbing against black asphalt. When he finally realized his car was trapped, he jumped out and ran.

My dad and Dr. Levenson tackled my brother in the driveway, where they held him down and forcibly maneuvered him into the backseat of the doctor's car. My mother stood motionless with her hand stuck over her open mouth, a statue of fear. I clutched the book of Zen quotes I was holding as if I could manually force the lessons of enlightenment into my horrified body.

Dr. Levenson tossed the keys out the car window to my mother. "You drive."

Snapped into action, gathering what little emotional strength she had left, my mom climbed into the driver's seat. As they pulled away I saw my brother in the back, kicking and screaming as my dad and Dr. Levenson restrained him.

Left alone in the fading light, I felt like one of the onlookers who, just that morning, had watched a stranger lead the police on a chase. Perhaps it was my homespun Zen practice of detachment kicking in or maybe the scene was just too big and surreal to grasp.

I stared at the sky painted beautifully by dusk, sun-streaked signature small in the right lower corner. I breathed in the twilight and let it soothe me. Then I walked back into the house, went to my room, and opened my book. I flipped the pages, stopping randomly, trusting that whatever quote I landed on would hold significance for me.

Hillary Carlip

"Accept the anxieties and difficulties of this life," I read. "Attain deliverance in disturbances."

I sat still for a while, not quite sure what to do next. Then I decided I didn't want to be alone. I had to get out of the house. I called my friend Karen, who was a year older than I was and had just gotten her driver's license. I asked if she wanted to go to a movie. I explained what had happened, and she said, "Wow. Well, since you've had a heavy day, I'm gonna let you choose the movie. I'll pick you up in fifteen."

"Cool."

I hung up, closed my eyes, and prayed for my brother, my mother, my father, and myself—that we would all attain deliverance in disturbances.

Then, in honor of my brother, in a hats-off to Howard's peyote button-induced psychedelic experiences of late, I decided we'd see *Fantasia*.

Karen picked me up, and as we drove to the theater I kept glancing behind us—just to make sure no one was following.

...IT CAME—FLOODING THE SCHOOLS, CRUSHING EVERYTHING THAT STOOD IN ITS WAY, LEAVING IN ITS WAKE A TRAIL OF DESTRUCTION, HAVOC, REBELLION. IT RAZED CLASSROOMS; FLINGING TEXTBOOKS TO THE WINDS, SCREAMING OUT OF TURN, LEAVING FOUL STAINS ON THE DESKS, RIPPING THE FLAGS FROM THEIR VERY POLES. IT CAUGHT SCORES OF STUDENTS, SWEEPING THEM ONWARD ON ITS HEADLONG COURSE, TRAPPING THEM IN THE WHIRLPOOL OF ITS FRENZY. ADMINISTRATORS REELED CHOKING ON ITS NOXIOUS REEK, AS IT TORE THEIR OFFICES ASUNDER. CUT SLIPS, TARDY SLIPS, SUSPENSION NOTICES, BAD CONDUCT NOTICES, REPORT CARDS—ALL WERE SWEPT AWAY IN ITS CHURNING MIST. IT WAS...

The

Vol 1 No. 3   HI SCHOOL COMMUNITY NEWS SERVICE   April 1972

Fall/Winter
1972

✳ Carly Simon marries James Taylor. Molly and I are not invited to the wedding. *Friends. Right.*

✳ The same week *Roe v. Wade* is reargued in Supreme Court, I go see the taping of the new show *Maude*. The episode is part one of the controversial "Maude's Dilemma," in which the forty-seven-year-old character decides to get an abortion. Despite protests, including pro-life groups mailing producer Norman Lear photographs of aborted fetuses, months later the Supreme Court rules that a woman's right to an abortion falls within the right to privacy protected by the Fourteenth Amendment, and abortion is legalized.

✳ The number one song is Helen Reddy's "I Am Woman." Right on.

✳ My two straight girlfriends Leslie and Dana sleep together and say they had an incredible, beautiful time. This helps me acknowledge my own repressed lesbian desires, even though I don't act on them yet.

✳ *The Joy of Sex* is released, featuring unsightly illustrations and watercolors of a very hairy heterosexual couple having sex. *Now* I act on my previously repressed lesbian desires and experience my first kiss with a girl.

✳ I am picked by lottery to attend my high school's alternative program. Students create our own classes and I get straight A's in Rose Breeding, Post-Sixties Novels, and Pantomime.

✳ As a volunteer, I help organize a McGovern for President benefit, where we show the film *Reefer Madness*.

✳ In the largest Republican landslide in history, Nixon defeats George McGovern. So much for us pot-smoking volunteers. . . .

✳ *Deliverance, Last Tango in Paris,* and *Pink Flamingos* are the big hit movies of the year, prompting nationwide dinnertime discussions about banjos, butter, and dog shit.

Adventures of a Teenage Woman Juggler

Carly Simon and Carole King were not the only talents I longed to emulate. I was also completely enamored with Lucille Ball and Carol Burnett, whose television shows I watched religiously from the edge of my parents' bed. I admired everything about these women, especially the way they made people laugh—*intentionally*. If they could do it maybe I could, too. But how?

The answer arrived one sticky summer day when I was hanging out at my friend Edwina Katzman's house. Edwina's parents had banished her older sister, Randi, to her olive green shag-carpeted bedroom—grounding her for breaking the large glass table in the dining room.

"How'd she break it?" I asked Edwina.

"Juggling," she laughed. "Can you believe it?"

Juggling? Throwing things in the air? I'd only seen jugglers on the *Ed Sullivan Show,* and they were always foreign men in spandex unitards. Girls juggled? Wow.

As if moved by a higher though possibly demented power, I flew upstairs to Randi's room and asked if she would teach me how to juggle. I don't know if she agreed to because she was bored to death after her week-long grounding or because I "paid" for my lesson by sneaking into her mother's nightstand drawer and pilfering four cigarettes for her.

Leaning against a musty-smelling patchwork quilt on Randi's bed, using three oranges I had fetched from the fruit bowl in the kitchen, Randi showed me the basic juggling pattern. I tried it and was surprised by how quickly it came to me. The oranges sailed through the air from my right hand to my left in neat, controllable arcs. There was no conscious awareness of how I was doing it—juggling just felt instinctual and effortless.

I was under five feet, over 140 pounds, and about as graceful as Don Knotts. When I didn't ditch gym, my schoolmates always picked me last for teams. But now, for the first time in all my fifteen years, I actually felt coordinated. It was an extraordinary moment.

While my mother's habit was martinis and Miltowns, my father's nicotine and work, and my brother's a variety of addictions from pot to potpies, I became obsessed with flinging objects into the air and catching them.

At home I practiced with oranges. Every time I dropped one, it would splatter on the floor, and my mother's toy poodle, Monkey, would stop her favorite activity—holding a furry slipper between her legs and wildly humping it—long enough to lick up the orange juice. Soon I realized that the reason Randi had taught me to juggle over her bed was that when the oranges dropped onto the quilt they stayed intact. So I stood over my own pouffy quilt patterned with pale pink and blue ballerinas—a handmade gift from Margarita, the older sister of Esperanza, our boarder from Guatemala—and for hours on end I juggled.

Catching and releasing in a smooth wave of grace, juggling was a meditation, something to focus on besides how uncomfortable I was with myself. I would come to find that it was also a distraction—people watched my juggling instead of *me*. And before long I started to feel like maybe I was worth watching.

Howard was now living with his therapist on a farm in Topanga

Canyon taking care of a family of peacocks, so my mother had a little more energy for me. On weekends she'd drive me to Westwood Village or the Los Angeles County Museum of Art and drop me off to work. I'd juggle on the streets beside acrobats, mimes, and other jugglers, who taught me how to "pass clubs"—throw fiberglass Indian pins back and forth to one another in elaborate patterns. We'd pass the hat for donations, and I'd hitch a ride back home, flop onto my bedroom floor, and spread out my loot—separating out the dollar bills, then counting pennies, nickels, dimes, and quarters and placing them into shiny piles like my very own teenage Fort Knox. I'd roll them all into brown paper cylinders that I'd picked up at the bank when I opened my own savings account with $3.75, and weekly I'd haul the rolls of change into the Westwood branch of Bank of America for deposit. While my friends were earning meager cash by babysitting or working at McDonald's, I was making enough money to buy records, concert tickets, and mystical books at the Bodhi Tree. I even raised money for the Los Angeles Women's Liberation Union and donated it to them by handing over the first $100 bill I had ever seen.

One night I went to a club on Melrose called the Ash Grove. Though a well-known a cappella singing group, the Persuasions, was headlining, as in the days of Carly and Carole, I'd come to see their opening act—the Obie Award–winning San Francisco Mime Troupe. Their name was misleading as they specialized in performing socially relevant theater with nary an imaginary rope pull in sight. But they *did* juggle.

After the show I found the dressing room and poked my head into the open door.

"Are you Hillary?" the only woman in the troupe asked.

"Yeah, you must be Jane."

"Great to finally meet you!" She startled me with a hug.

"You too," I said, awkwardly hugging her back. "Your show was incredible!"

Since there weren't many professional female jugglers in the country, Jane and I had been corresponding after reading about each other in the International Juggler's Association newsletter. Before she said another word, Jane picked up a large green duffel bag, grabbed my hand, and dragged me to the stage. The audience had left, and waitresses were noisily clearing off tables.

Jane pulled some equipment out of her bag. "Let's pass clubs."

This, I'd discovered over the six months since I'd begun juggling, was a common greeting between jugglers—an instant connection that replaced small talk. Jane and I began to toss the pins to each other, and one by one three men from her troupe seamlessly joined in, never interrupting the pattern.

The owner of the club, a middle-aged man who smelled like smoke, watched us with fascination. "You guys were great tonight. How soon can I get you back here for another gig?"

Never taking her eyes off the pins flying through the air like fiberglass torpedoes, Jane coolly answered, "We're booked for the rest of the year, touring the country with our act."

I wanted to be able to say those words. And with Jane's self-assurance. *Touring. With my act.* Only problem was, I had no act. But juggling gave me balls. Without thinking I blurted out, "I live in town. I could perform."

The club owner laughed. "I'm not gonna ask how old you are. You know we serve liquor?"

I sighed heavily, defeated by my adolescence. But to my surprise the owner smiled and said, "Well, I can't really hire you, but what if you juggled between the opening acts and headliners? You could pass the hat."

"Perf." I tried to sound as laid-back as possible. After all, I was about to become a *true* professional. "I'll start next week."

At home that evening I began to write my first comedy juggling routine. With Lucy and Carol as my muses, I stayed up for three nights fueled by Mystic Mints and Dr Pepper, writing and rewriting my act on lined notebook paper. I tried it out on my mom and dad, who thought it was pretty good. Well, "cute" is what they called it. I decided I needed musical accompaniment and convinced Greg to be my pianist, even though he didn't know how to play the piano. He made up one abstract, circus-sounding song, memorized it, and one week later "Hillary the Woman Juggler" began performing regularly at the Ash Grove. I'd juggle before such headliners as Linda Ronstadt, Lightnin' Hopkins, Ramblin' Jack Elliot, and Maria "Midnight at the Oasis" Muldaur.

One night I was about to do my act before jazz legend Pharaoh Sanders's set. The audience was classy, older, and predominantly black. I felt anxious—I was the only fifteen-year-old white girl in the room, except for Greg, who was so effeminate he might as well have been a white girl.

Well, I thought, why not use the uncomfortable situation—play on it. I slipped into the dressing room and borrowed a guitar case from the opening act's guitarist. I placed my juggling balls in the case. When it was time for me to go on, I walked toward the stage, past men drinking bourbon and women smoking Virginia Slims; no one paid any attention to me. Greg followed and sat down at the piano. The lights dimmed, and the emcee introduced me, leaving off "juggler" as I had asked him to.

The audience grew quiet. But when the lights came back up and the crowd saw me onstage, dressed in my Indian print bell-bottoms with a rust-colored wraparound leotard and carrying the guitar case, they instantly grew restless. These were hard-core elite jazz enthusiasts waiting to see a musician who had performed his own genre of "Nubian Space Jazz" with Sun Ra and John Coltrane.

Greg began the song, and the crowd started to boo. The "boos" grew louder as I put the guitar case down and opened it. I started shaking. Part of me wanted to vanish into my safe, familiar world of juggling oranges over my ballerina bedspread, but I thought of Lucy Ricardo; whenever Lucy wanted to make something happen there was no stopping her. I summoned Lucy's determination as I pulled three hot pink balls out of the guitar case. I began to juggle. Within a few seconds the crowd quieted and began to watch me. My plan had worked. At least a teenage white girl in a leotard *juggling* was better than a teenage white girl in a leotard *playing guitar*.

Then I launched into my comic patter—a story I'd written about working at a bakery, using juggling tricks as puns. "I have a lot on my mind" I said as I rolled the balls off my head; "I've had ups and downs" (I tossed the balls up and down in columns). I squinted into the spotlight, focusing on the fluorescent pink orbs sailing through the air. I looked into the crowd and caught one older gentleman's eye. When he slowly nodded approvingly, I felt encouraged, and I forged on, the tricks becoming more complex, the puns more groan-evoking.

"To make bread, you *knead* . . . " I said, bouncing the balls off my knees.

"You can't be *blind* to what the customer wants . . . " (I rolled the balls across eyes).

"My co-workers and I really *hit it off* . . . " (I hit one ball consecutively off my elbow, forearm, back of hand).

The audience began to laugh and applaud. I left the hardest trick for last. "Working at the bakery is a *pain in the neck*," I said as I threw a ball out of the pattern above my head, squatted, flattening my back just in time to catch the ball in the crook of my neck. The crowd let loose with cheers. Then I whipped back up, and the ball flew out and over my head, returning to the juggling pattern. Greg played our climactic finish, running his hand from top key to bottom. Black, white, old, young—none of that mattered any longer. The crowd went wild. They gave me a standing ovation.

My dreams were no longer on hold. Finally I was making people laugh—*intentionally*.

After that I performed at the club every week, sometimes with Greg, most times alone. I was applauded and lauded, and I almost keeled over with joy when I read my first review, a rave in the *Los Ange-*

les Times. A week later, I bought up all copies of the *Herald-Examiner* at every newsstand within five miles from my house because a reviewer wrote: "Amazing. . . . Hillary has to be seen to be believed. . . . She deserved ten encores. . . . "

But while the opening and headlining acts hung out with each other, I sat alone in the dressing room, sipping virgin peach daiquiris, no one talking to me. I teetered between two disparate worlds—high school and the L.A. nightclub scene—and I belonged to neither.

For the next seven months I continued my gig at the Ash Grove, until one windy October night its name proved prophetic, and the club burned to the ground.

I was distraught. Since I'd experienced the luxury of performing onstage, I couldn't bear to return to the streets. But what other club would hire an underaged schoolgirl to juggle between acts? I was soon to find out—*none*. I pondered my future, only then realizing that making a living from juggling was going to be a challenge.

And then one winter afternoon, providence came to me over chili-cheese fries at an Orange Julius. That's where I found a brochure for a Learning Annex type of program called Heliotrope. Through this Open University people taught all kinds of classes out of their homes: "Advanced Macramé"; "Creative Casseroles." Why not juggling?

I was sure the description I wrote for the catalog—including the enticing phrase, "Let me help you fulfill your fondest fantasies"—would surely seal the deal for those trying to decide between my class and "How to Make Giant Tissue Paper Flowers." In fact since I knew "Learn to Juggle" would be in such high demand, and I'd fulfill my maximum of ten students, I xeroxed ten copies of a handout I had created, complete with hand-drawn diagrams of juggling patterns.

When I received the call from Heliotrope informing me that only one person had signed up, I was totally bummed. But since I was holding the juggling class in my tiny bedroom and hadn't really considered how more than two people would fit, I figured it was just as well.

On the first night of class I asked my parents to make themselves scarce. "Who's coming over?" my dad asked.

"Heliotrope only told me his name is Bob."

"Well, I'm sticking around to check him out," Dad said.

"All right," I agreed, "but Mom, *please* make sure Monkey's locked in your bedroom." I couldn't deal with the possibility that my mom's poodle would be humping the furry slipper when my student arrived.

My father was an ex-artist whose insatiable interior design hobby caused him to redecorate the house every few months. He had recently painted our entire downstairs a dramatic black, so when I heard the doorbell ring, I raced around turning on every light. Then I ran to the door and opened it to find my pupil standing there: a stocky older man with a gray goatee.

"Hi," he said. "I'm Bob."

"I'm Hillary. Come in."

He stepped into the foyer, and my dad walked in from the kitchen.

"Hi Bob, I'm Bob Carlip." He extended his arm, and the two men shook hands.

I looked at my dad with a See? He's fine. My dad pulled me aside for just a second and whispered, "Leave your door open."

Bob seemed older than both my parents, but since I was the teacher, I said in my most authoritative tone, "All right, Bob. Let's get goin'."

He followed me up the stairs. After months of living with his therapist, Howard had just moved back home, so I pretended not to notice the smoke seeping from beneath his door, forming a pot-scented cloud in the hallway. Once in my bedroom, I picked up three balls that sat on the Guatemalan-made ballerina quilt on my twin bed, and began the first lesson of our four-week class. Step by step, ball by ball, I showed Bob the basic juggling pattern, leading him in proper arcing, tossing, and catching. I was reassured when two hours later, at the end of our first class, Bob smiled and said, "That was great. See you next week."

When he returned for the following lesson, Bob told me he was a television writer. Learning to juggle, he explained, was research for his work.

"Neat," I said. "Have you written for any show I might have seen?"

"Probably," he answered casually. *"I Love Lucy, The Lucy Show, Here's Lucy."*

My heart started beating so loudly, the sound drowned out Hendrix blasting from my brother's room. Bob, this ordinary old man juggling in my bedroom, worked on a daily basis with my idol. I'd seen his credit roll into that *I Love Lucy* heart a thousand times.

"You're Bob Carroll Jr.?"

"That would be me," he said. "I'm learning to juggle so I can teach Lucy."

No. Way.

"Lucy has to learn how to do something really well before she can make it look like she doesn't know how to do it at all."

"Like the time when she was trying to climb into the top bunk bed with the stilts?"

"Exactly." He beamed, clearly impressed with my episodic knowledge.

"Well," I sputtered, the wheels turning, "Lucy really could learn more effectively if I taught her directly. I could stop by the set or something."

Bob smiled. "She's just so busy, it's hard to pin down a time with her. I'm going to show her whenever we can just grab a second."

"I see." Oh well, I tried.

Over the next two weeks Bob proved to be an excellent student. On the night of his final class he said, "Lucy's going to be very excited. She really does want to learn how to juggle."

A strange calm oozed through me like taking that first sip of hot chocolate on a chilly night and feeling it pulse through your veins. For so long I'd wanted to be like Lucy. Now Lucy wanted to be like me.

I saw Bob to the door, where he gave me a strong, fatherly hug. By then I felt so confident, I didn't even care that in the foyer where we said good-bye, Monkey was humping the slipper.

iotrope
PEN UNIVERSITY

B-21: LEARN TO JUGGLE: $10
Hillary carlip   west l.a.
Have you ever dreamed of leaving it all
and running off to the circus? Well now all
can! Let me help you fulfill your fondest
fantasies. Come learn how to juggle! I will
teach you ball juggling (various variations)
clubs, rings, or whatever comes, etc.
torches, stars, ice cream cones, etc.)
individual attention given. I will teach you
on your own level. By the first lesson you'll
be able to juggle!

meetings: Wednesdays 7 - 9 pm. starting
FEBRUARY 7. Class size 4-10.

International Jugglers
HAS ACCEPTED

Hillary Carlip

AS A MEMBER
IN
GOOD STANDING

FOR THE YEAR

1973

Lucille Ball Productions, Inc.
UNIVERSAL STUDIOS
UNIVERSAL CITY, CALIFORNIA 91608

1976

✳ While attending college at the University of California at Santa Cruz, I write papers in longhand for classes such as Ritual Theater and Sexuality in the Cinema. Meanwhile, Apple releases its first computer, and a little-known company called Microsoft registers its trade name with the Office of the Secretary of the State of New Mexico.

✳ I set off the fire alarm in my dorm by eating fire, and cause a full-scale evacuation.

✳ George H.W. Bush begins his one-year stint as the director of the CIA as *Charlie's Angels* begin their five-year stint as smart and sexy crime-fighters.

* Patty "Tanya" Hearst is convicted of armed robbery and Sara Jane Moore is sentenced to life for attempting to shoot President Ford. Though "Bad Girls" won't be a hit for Donna Summer for a few years, her song "Love to Love You Baby" tops the charts.

* My gloom over not being in a relationship is magnified when everyone else seems to be in one—Captain and Tennille, Bianca and Mick, and even Sonny and Cher, who, though divorced, reunite for the new *Sonny and Cher Show*.

* Shortly after attending "Gay Day" at Ho Chi Minh Park in Berkeley, I meet my first real girlfriend. *Finally*, some "Afternoon Delight"!

* O. J. Simpson gains 273 yards for Buffalo vs. Detroit while the Supreme Court lifts the 1972 ban on the death penalty for convicted murderers.

* After having done the EST training I continue taking workshops, including a weekend seminar in L.A. called "Communication in Performing Arts" where, during an exercise, I am partnered with Valerie Harper, star of *Rhoda*.

* I leave college and move to New York for six months to pursue my career as an entertainer. I perform at the Grove Street Playhouse—where I juggle and eat fire along with future MacArthur genius grant recipient Michael Moschen—as the Son of Sam terrorizes the city.

Queen of the Oddballs

I sit anxiously in a waiting room, sandwiched between an enormously overweight woman dressed like a chicken and an old toothless fiddler. A wiry, bearded man standing in front of me deeply inhales a cigar, then blows smoke rings into different shapes—hearts, squares, crosses—while a young black woman in an ill-fitting, peach-colored suit bursts into riffs as if she's testifying to Lord Jesus. I'm a nineteen-year-old chubby girl squeezed into a black sequined gown with a fur wrap draped over my shoulders and carrying three juggling balls in a gold lamé purse. So who am I to judge?

Although we are all chatty and sweet to one another, in truth we're fierce competitors. After all, only one of us can win *The Gong Show*.

We're moments away from taping in front of a live studio audience when in walks Chuck Barris, the lovable, bumbling host who years later, in his autobiographical tell-all book and subsequent movie, *Confessions of a Dangerous Mind*, will reveal that he's a CIA assassin.

"Hey everybody." He claps his hands, shifting from one foot to the other. "We've got a lot of great stuff today. So just have fun." His mischievous smile is endearing and his messy hair comforting, despite the fact that he may have just returned from offing someone.

The taping begins. Smoke-ring guy is the first one called to the stage. The rest of us watch the show on a monitor in the beige Green Room. This is the first time we're seeing the acts we're up against, and I am at once relieved and frightened to discover that most of the oddballs I've been hanging out with all day are not just talentless, they're utterly delusional.

But wait. Do they think I'm like them? No way. I'm a professional. I've been reviewed—the *Herald-Examiner* said I deserved ten encores, the *Los Angeles Times* thought I was doing important work, and the *Santa Cruz Sentinel* called me extraordinary! Shit—maybe appearing on *The Gong Show* isn't the career move I thought it would be. What if millions of people watching think I'm deluded, too? Worse—*what if I get gonged*? I take a deep breath, trying to calm myself down without inhaling too much of old toothless fiddler's B.O.

Smoke-ring guy receives a score of fourteen out of a possible thirty. Next up is big, fat, chicken lady whose act consists of telling bad "why did the chicken cross the road" jokes and after each one, belting out "SQUAWK." She's not gonged by just one of the judges, she's gonged by *all three*. Dejected, she returns to the green room and exclaims, "I got gang-gonged."

But the old fiddler, who is up next, takes me by surprise. Not only does he give a kick-ass performance, he's so damn cute playing "Turkey in the Straw" and flashing his toothless smile that when the judges give him twenty-nine out of thirty points, I'm thrilled. That is until I realize *he* now has the score *I* have to beat. By the time the producer calls my name I am so nervous, sweat has gathered under my politically correct unshaven armpits.

A masculine woman wearing a headset leads me to the stage and instructs me to wait behind the curtain for my cue. I hear the stage manager's countdown "five, four, three, two. . . . " and Milton Delugg and the *Gong Show* band strike up the familiar *Gong Show* theme song. I've watched Chuck Barris doing his shticky intros countless times, but this one's *for me*. I listen intently.

"This next act will have you holding your breath. She has a great act but a lousy perfume. Let's hear it for Hillary Carlip!"

Oh my God. That's *got to be* a random intro. He can't smell me from out there, can he? Just before the curtain rises I quickly wipe the sweat from my armpits with the end of my fake-fur wrap. I carry a chair onto the stage and set it down. I sing the intro to my song, which I originally wrote as an audition piece for a musical comedy workshop at my college, the University of California at Santa Cruz, led by the famed satirist Tom Lehrer. He didn't accept me into the workshop, but Tom and I did form a friendship, and it was he who helped me rewrite the song to perfection—the song I'm performing and *could get gonged for* on national TV.

I set my purse down on the chair and peel off my jacket, revealing my sequined gown. The audience "oohs" and "aaahs." They have no idea what's coming as I open my gold lamé purse and pull out three bright orange juggling balls.

I sing my song, "I Really Get a Kick When He's Around," accompanying each lyric with a coordinating juggling trick, a variation on my original bakery routine. When I sing "kick," I kick the ball off my foot, without interrupting the pattern. The audience eagerly leans forward as I sing, "He does things behind my back" and send the balls there. By the time I reach "Our love is a bust" and roll the balls over my chest, the crowd is in hysterics, and I'm gaining confidence since the showstopper is yet to come.

I slow down the verse and launch into, "And then when I tell him to watch-it-he . . . tells me I'm just being crotchety . . ." and you can guess where the balls go on that line. The audience and judges howl, forcing the band to vamp until the laughter dies down.

I finish my routine and return the balls to my purse. I am so relieved to have made it through the whole song without dropping a ball—or getting gonged—that when Chuck Barris moves toward me, arms outstretched, I lean in to give him a great big hug.

I can't stop smiling—not because I'm relieved, but because my extra-dry top lip is sticking to my gums. Chuck turns to the judges. "So, what do you all think of Hillary Carlip?"

Elke Sommer, the foxy Fraulein destined for *Love Boat* guest star status, shouts: "Fabulous! I give her a ten!"

Next, the sassy, saucy songstress Jaye P. Morgan says, "You're sensational. You do everything right," and I receive my second perfect ten.

I wait, my left leg shaking, as the last judge weighs in. Cocky critic Rex Reed, *Gong Show* regular, has never given anyone a ten, but that's what I'll need to beat ol' kick-ass, toothless fiddler. Everything around me begins to move in slow motion.

"I thought you were terrific," Rex says. "I love the way you sing. I have a reputation on this show for being the mean old man of the panel. This is the very first time I have ever given a ten."

I hold in the screech that threatens to burst out of my fur-wrapped throat as the audience cheers. I return to the Green Room, where I expect to be greeted with cool, competitive snubs, but everyone showers me with warm congratulations.

"That was fantastic!" Chicken Lady squawks as she hugs me.

"Spectacular," croaks an eighty-six-year-old woman wearing a silver sequined minidress and a huge pink bow on top of bleached blond hair.

Even old toothless fiddler, whom I now have officially beaten, pats me on the back and lisps, "Marvelouth!"

I can't help but be moved by my fellow contestants, who rather than hide their oddness, *celebrate* it.

We sit together and watch the monitor, where we can see the next contestant perform. It's the young black woman in the ill-fitting, peach-colored suit, and she's singing the hell out of "You Are So Beautiful." Shit. She's good. Really good.

When the judges weigh in Elke and Jaye P. each give the woman a ten. And now that I've opened the dam on Rex Reed's generosity, he gives her his second-ever ten.

We suddenly have . . . *a tie.*

I haven't been this nervous since my last TV performance, two years ago, when I taught tennis sensation Jimmy Connors how to juggle on Dinah Shore's TV show *Dinah!*

Hillary Carlip

At the end of the taping, as all the contestants are ushered onto the stage, the huge woman dressed like a chicken takes me under her wing, figuratively and literally. The audience must break the tie by a show of applause.

My competition is first. Chuck Barris puts his hand over her head. "Let's hear it for Cheryl Lynn!"

The audience applauds wildly. They love her. I'm sweating more than ever. Chuck places his hand over my head. "Now, Hillary Carlip!" The cheering swells. The "applause-o-meter" soars.

I've just won *The Gong Show*.

Milton Delugg and the band strike up the theme song, Chuck Barris kisses me on the lips, balloons tumble from the ceiling, and a midget scurries onstage and tosses confetti from a basket. Siv Aberg, the gorgeous, Swedish *Gong Show* hostess, presents me with the trophy and a Publisher's Clearing House-like, jumbo-sized check for $712.05.

The judges walk onstage and give me congratulatory kisses. The sassy, saucy Jaye P. Morgan gives me an extra-long hug and a lingering, direct-eye-contact look. Is Jaye P. Morgan cruising me? Before I can explore this further, the confetti-tossing midget grabs me and leads me in a demented, high-speed waltz.

In all the hubbub, I notice a dejected Cheryl Lynn. I walk over, take her hand, and tell her how amazing she was. A few months later, I read in *People* magazine that the day after our show airs, Cheryl Lynn is contacted by the president of Columbia Records, who signs her to a major record deal. Not long after, she rises to the top of the charts with her hugely successful disco hit song, "Got to Be Real."

But today I am the winner. And not just because I prevailed over future disco sensation Cheryl Lynn. I also won a high-speed waltz with a confetti-tossing midget, a kiss on the lips from a professed CIA assassin, a hug from a lady dressed like a chicken, and a pat on the back from an old toothless fiddler. I am surrounded by a posse of oddballs, and today I am the Queen.

Summer
1980

✻ I am hired to teach Jimmie "J. J." Walker—wisecracking, "DY-NO-MITE"-spouting star of the hit TV show *Good Times*—how to juggle.

✻ While people use the first portable listening device recently introduced to the United States—the Sony Walkman—to listen to Captain and Tenille's "Do That to Me One More Time" and Rupert Holmes's "Escape (The Pina Colada Song)," I'm listening to Siouxsie and the Banshees' "Christine" and X's "Los Angeles."

✻ President Carter leads a boycott of the Summer Olympics in Moscow to protest the Soviet invasion of Afghanistan. Decades later, there are protests when President Bush invades Afghanistan.

✻ I lose twenty pounds on the Scarsdale diet shortly after Dr. Herman Tarnower, the creator of the diet, loses his life when his jilted lover, Jean Harris, bumps him off.

✻ The new toy Rubik's Cube is in such high demand that it's as difficult to buy as it is to solve.

✻ I go several times to Chippendales, one of L.A.'s most popular nightclubs, to see their hot, all-male, dancing stripper revue.

* *The David Letterman Show*, a morning talk show, runs for just three months on NBC before being cancelled. Guess Letterman's not really talk show material.

* I am obsessed with watching the Z Channel, one of the first cable TV movie channels devoted to screening rare classics, important foreign films, and American titles that have fallen through the cracks of commercial distribution.

* I perform my *Gong Show*–winning comedy juggling song at clubs and theaters along with my piano accompanist—*Michael Feinstein*.

Dear Olivia Newton-John

8/8/80

Dear Olivia Newton-John:

Let me say what a pleasure it was working with you on *Xanadu*! Remember, I was the dancer wearing the twenties bathing suit in the "All Over the World" number (I know—what the hell was the costumer thinking?), and I was also in white face (again, not my idea!) when I juggled in the big Xanadu nightclub finale. After spending more than a month filming together every day, I think we know each other well enough for me to call you Livvy.

So Livvy, I'm writing this now because I've just come from the premiere screening of our movie. It transported me back ten months to the shoot, and when I got home, I realized I owed you a long-overdue thank-you note.

That's right, Livvy, THANK YOU! Because whether you know it or not, you gave me some valuable advice on the set of *Xanadu*, advice that has had an enormous impact on my love life. Oh, and not because you're a lesbian! Despite the rampant rumors, I don't believe you're gay. Remember, I witnessed you and my fellow dancer, Matt Lattanzi, get together on the set! Damn, were we all shocked—I mean whoever thought some twenty-one-year-old boy, eleven years younger than you (don't get me wrong—you look fabulous!) would score with you? You were just so totally out of his league.

But anyway, let me explain why a thank-you is in order. See, when I was cast in *Xanadu,* I had *just* moved to L.A. Before that I had been living in San Francisco for two years where, besides performing, I was busy marching in demonstrations and hanging out with women who didn't shave, who believed fat was a feminist issue, and who thought makeup objectified women and kept them under the patriarchal rule. In fact, I was one of those women!

My girlfriend, Daisy, decided to move to L.A. with me. She was my first long-term relationship, despite the fact that she had had several affairs while we were together—including a tryst with a female friend of ours and a wild night with our male next-door neighbor. At first everything was fine in L.A. We moved into a cute little duplex in the Hollywood Hills. But then I started getting jobs, and she couldn't find one. I had my own car and friends; she had *my* car and friends. She quickly became resentful and I was still distrustful. But Livvy, we did love each other and we tried to make our relationship work.

And then came *Xanadu.* Let me tell you, that first day when I walked onto the set at Fiorucci, where you took Gene Kelly to buy an outfit for the big opening of the nightclub, I could hardly catch my breath when I saw all those gorgeous dancers. I'd never set eyes on so many amazing-looking women all in one place.

Then the shooting began—those fourteen-hour days, all those people having affairs with each other (you included, Liv!). It was tempting, but I lived with someone, and just because she had cheated on me didn't mean I was going to do the same. Besides, I had never gone after any of my relationships—since I wouldn't dare take the chance of being rejected, I always let others pursue me. And although I was putting together a style that was a little more interesting than my who-gives-a-shit-how-I-look fashion in San Francisco, it was obvious that none of those beautiful dancers were going to be beating down my dressing room door!

Meanwhile Daisy finally got a job (she's a hairdresser), and started making her own friends at the salon. We both were so busy, we almost never saw each other during the week, and on weekends we'd try to reconnect. But even when we went out to dinner or to a movie, we were feeling really strained. One Sunday when we were cleaning the house, Daisy turned off the vacuum and said, "Maybe we'd be happier if we had an open relationship. Whaddya think?"

Wow. She was already sort of doing that anyway, so I said, "Sure, let's try it."

"I think you should have an affair," Daisy added, and then she returned to vacuuming the hallway. I swear, I'm not making this up. There was my girlfriend, urging me to have an affair!

So back at work we finished shooting the "All Over the World" number at Fiorucci and moved over to the soundstage at Hollywood General Studios to shoot the BIG XANADU FINALE! On our first day at the studio, a few of the dancers were rehearsing part of the production number without you, Livvy. I was watching this inner circle of boy dancers facing an outer circle of girl dancers. Each boy would twirl his girl, and then the girl circle would move one step right so that a new girl stood in front of that boy. Then he would twirl her, and so on. You remember that routine, don't you?

I was standing there, leaning against a pillar and wondering if the girls felt dizzy with all that twirling going on, when suddenly I spotted her. A GORGEOUS, striking dancer with sandy red hair, radiant green eyes, and a sexiness that exuded in spite of (or maybe *because* of?!) the baggy overalls she was wearing to rehearse in. She looked like a young Ann-Margret from her *Kitten with a Whip* days. I'd noticed her at Fiorucci, too, but there she'd been just one of the bevy of beautiful dancers. What made her stand out now was that she was *in the boys' circle*, twirling one girl, and then another, and then another. Come on, Livvy, even if you're not gay, you have to admit that was *totally hot!*

So I stood there thinking, hmm, Daisy says I should have an affair. Well, why not with this girl? *Yeah, right.* Like she's even gay. Just because she's dancing with other women, it's choreographed that way. And even if by any remote chance she *is* gay, like I'm ever going to pursue a totally stunning dancer I'm sure to be rejected by? No way!

By now you're probably trying to remember the advice you gave me, Livvy. I'm getting there in a sec! So even though that gorgeous girl dancer was completely out of my league (like you were to Matt, see where I'm going?), I had to find out who she was, and I guess Fate played a little part in this because I happened to ask the perfect person: Nick, one of my fellow jugglers, who was standing nearby.

"That's Celeste," he answered with a grin. "Did you ever meet my ex-girlfriend Danielle? She manages Fiorucci."

"No."

Nick leaned in close and whispered, "A couple of years ago Danielle left me for Celeste."

Livvy, I almost fainted.

Okay. Here's where you come in. As we rehearsed over the next couple of days, your song for the finale played again and again and again—hundreds of times a day. Over and over, your words (sung so beautifully, I might add) hypnotically planted the suggestion in my brain:

You have to believe we are magic, nothing can stand in our way
You have to believe we are magic, don't let your aim ever stray
And if all your hopes survive, destiny will arrive
I'll bring all your dreams alive . . . for you.

Because of your lyrics, Liv, I was determined to believe that *I* was magic, let nothing stand in my way, and trust that I could bring all my dreams alive . . . for me! Too bad I wasn't dreaming of a huge career break or financial freedom or world peace and justice for all. I was intent on pursuing, wooing, and scoring a dancer on *Xanadu*.

I decided that during the eleven remaining days of shooting, I would make some sort of move toward Celeste daily.

Hillary Carlip

DAY 1: I walked up to Celeste and told her she was great in the twirling number. She said thanks and turned away.

DAY 2: I smiled at Celeste and asked how her weekend was. "Nice, thanks," she said, and turned away.

DAY 3: I befriended Mandy, you remember her, the one who did that killer swing dance with her partner? She was Celeste's friend, and I figured if Celeste saw that Mandy thought I was cool, she might, too. (I really liked Mandy, so it wasn't entirely scheming!)

DAY 4: When I saw Celeste writing in a notebook, I sauntered over and asked if she could spare a piece of paper. This time I said, "I'm Hillary, by the way."

She said, "Hi, I'm Celeste," and we chatted for about three minutes. Actually, I think it was about you and Matt! I tried to be as charming as possible.

DAY 5: In the morning we said hello, and smiled at each other during the day. In fact, several times she caught me looking at her, and a few other times I caught her looking at me. And whenever either of us caught the other looking, we'd quickly turn away. I seemed to be making progress!

DAY 6: I knew Celeste would be at a party one of the dancers was throwing, so I put together my best outfit, which included a black bowling shirt with "Betty" embroidered in red over the pocket. I felt sorta cute at the party until I laid eyes on Celeste. She was wearing a sixties minidress, the bottom black- and white-striped and the top a lime green material, with a green bow around her narrow dancer's waist. Her vintage black patent leather spiked heels matched her purse, and she wore sixties makeup with the eyeliner extending into cat eyes. She looked unbelievably, stylishly, fabulously, extraordinarily, well, unbelievable! We smiled at each other from across the room, but an hour passed with no contact. Finally when I saw she was getting tipsy, I made my way over to her. We talked awhile, and then she suggested we go together on a "mission" to capture a bottle of wine and sneak out to my car with it.

"Oh, but there are obstacles," she declared, pointing at Lonny, "an international spy who has been tailing me throughout Europe and the States." The ruse went on, becoming more complex, and I joined in, pulling her away to hide from Tanya, her "angry ex-girlfriend who can't see us together or there will be hell to pay."

We agreed we must remain cool and discreet. Celeste touched the pocket of my bowling shirt. "Code name: Betty," she whispered.

I smiled at my own beautiful Ann-Margret and said, "Code name: Ann."

We were officially partners in crime.

I knew right away that "Ann" was a madwoman. As she drank another glass of wine, an edge surfaced. She was the type whose hostility and bitterness lash out unedited when they're drunk. But she was gorgeous, creative, and totally fun, so I was thrilled when she sent her friends home, telling them she'd get a ride with me.

By the end of our mission we were sitting in my car swigging white wine from the bottle. Well *she* was. I don't really like alcohol, and someone had to drive, so I kept pretending to sip because I could tell that she didn't want this night to end and, of course, neither did I.

At 3:30 a.m. we went to Canter's restaurant. When we strolled in we ran into several people we knew, and joined their table. Others arrived and with each new arrival, "Ann" and I were pushed closer together. By sunrise, when I dropped her off at home and she hugged me good-bye, I was drunk on her perfume, which I later learned was, naturally, Ambush.

I climbed into bed as Daisy was climbing out to go to work. I told her I'd been out with a bunch of people from the film, figuring there was no sense letting her know that my every nerve ending was electrified and I couldn't shake the scent of Ambush out of my head.

DAY 7: It was dark and pouring rain all Monday. I wasn't scheduled to work, and it took everything in me not to stop by the set anyway.

DAY 8: I saw Celeste first thing in the morning, and although I greeted her warmly, she was frosty and distant. Shit. Maybe she realized I was interested in her and this was her way of showing me she didn't return the feelings? Most of the day I didn't see Celeste—she was rehearsing a number with you, Livvy, while the other jugglers and I were working on the bit where we passed clubs over your co-stars' heads as they entered the nightclub under the arch of our pattern. That evening, when we wrapped for the day, I asked Mandy and a few other girls if they wanted to go out for a drink. Mandy invited Celeste (as I'd hoped she would!). On the way out of the studio, Celeste walked over and uttered her first words to me all day: "You comin', Betty?"

"Yeah, I am, Ann."

From that moment on, we referred to each other only as Ann and Betty.

Six of us sat around a table at the Gold Coast bar in West Hollywood talking about who was sleeping with who on the set, when Ann excused herself to go to the ladies room. As she stood up, she kicked me under the table and subtly motioned with her head for me to follow.

I waited the longest minute of my life then excused myself. Just as I approached the door it creaked open, and Ann extended an arm and yanked me inside. She pushed me against a wall and began to kiss me furiously. We couldn't keep our hands—or our mouths—off each other. Frenzied, heavy-breathed excitement mixed with slow, deep exploration, nails digging into skin, tongues swirling, lips smothering.

Twenty minutes later when we finally returned to the table, the others laughed and gave us knowing looks.

"What?" Ann asked. "There were people in line, we had to wait."

Later, in the parking lot, we waved good-bye to our friends, and the moment they were gone, Ann and I lunged for each other. We leaned against her car, a brilliant 1961 black and yellow Metropolitan with plaid seats, and began to make out some more.

A policeman walked by. We stopped. When he was out of sight, we moved a few rows down to my car and continued to kiss. The cop walked by again. We ducked. Everything about Ann was thrilling and dangerous.

That night I decided to come clean with Daisy—well, maybe not full-on shower clean, but at least sponge-bath clean. I told her I had met someone I was *thinking* about having an affair with.

"Good," she said.

I could tell Daisy was pissed, though she didn't have the right to say anything more. She sort of swallowed hard and said, "By the way, remember the other night when I came home so late? I slept with a guy from work."

"You what?" I yelped. I couldn't believe it.

"I mean we decided it'd be okay, didn't we?"

I caught my breath, which had gone missing when she delivered the blow, then decided to see this as my chance to be with Ann. "Fine. Yeah, we did," I answered.

DAY 9: Another day off for me. As it was nearing Christmas, days were getting colder, but this day was rain-free. I bundled up in a heavy coat and scarf, packed a picnic, drove to the set at lunchtime, and picked up Ann. Off we went to a nearby park that was full of cholos drinking beer, mothers gossiping, and children screaming as they played, so we couldn't exactly continue where we'd left off last night. We talked instead.

"This is all pretty intense," I said.

"Yeah, I know."

"What are we gonna do about it?"

"I'm not sure." Ann knitted her brow. "I just wasn't planning on this. . . . "

Of course she wasn't. This was all your doing, Livvy!

"And, well, you should know. . . ." Ann picked at a baguette and tossed crumbs to nearby robins. "I have a girlfriend."

Damn. Now what? Maybe I should just stop while I was ahead? After all, I'd proven I could actually pursue a woman who was seemingly out of my league and succeed. What more did I want?

And then it occurred to me. Maybe the fact that she was with someone made this even easier. I could do what Daisy was encouraging—just have *an affair*. Daisy had managed to do that and remain "hopelessly devoted" (get it?!) to me. Why couldn't I?

"Perfect," I told her. "I have a girlfriend, too."

That night Daisy pushed and prodded. "Details, I want details," she said. So I gave her *some* details. And what did she do? She freaked out. "Everyone I've slept with has been just about sex," she shouted. "There wasn't any emotional connection, but I can tell."

"You can tell what?"

"You're totally into this girl."

Then she stormed into the guest bedroom and slept there.

Oh, Livvy, I guess you didn't address the hard part of "magic" in your song!

DAY 10: We started to shoot the juggling scene—that's when I had to wear that cheesy white mime makeup. And Livvy, we all know that mimes are anything but sexy. I can vouch for that cuz the first guy I really made out with when I was in junior high school was a professional mime, and kissing him made me gag.

So, understandably, Ann kept her distance. During the lunch break I didn't see her at all, so I was convinced she had totally withdrawn again. Later in the day shooting began on the roller skating part of the finale, which neither of us were in. I was hanging out, talking to some friends, trying to decide whether or not to approach Ann, when she beat me to it.

"Betty, can you help me with my costume for a minute?"

"Sure."

She was wearing a slinky black dress that looked more than fine to me.

"I think there's a safety pin in one of the trailers," she said, all blasé, acting like we were pals and nothing at all had ever happened between us. She led me through the lot into a trailer that was empty except for a dresser, a mirror, and the late afternoon sun pouring in through a small window, casting a spotlight on . . . A BED.

Ann pushed me into the sun's rays and climbed on top of me. Her lips consumed mine. We kissed for what seemed like an eternity but at the same time only a second. When we finally came up for air, we both began to laugh. Her impeccable makeup was blotted with white mime paint; my face was one big smear.

"What if we're called to shoot?" I asked.

"How can we be called to shoot," she said devilishly, "when no one knows where we are?"

The responsible, don't-let-anyone-down, do-the-right-thing girl in me disappeared when Ann grabbed me again, continuing our three-way with the sun.

That weekend Daisy decided to get away to San Francisco. I was thrilled to have the opportunity to see Ann, but despite leaving her two messages, I didn't hear back from her all weekend. I assumed she was with her girlfriend, and I tried not to let that disturb me.

I began to wonder what would happen when, after the next day, our last day of shooting, Ann and I weren't around each other every day. Liv, I should have asked you to tell me more about movie-set flings. But I guess whatever you might have said wouldn't have mattered. I was already hooked.

Hillary Carlip

DAY 11: Ann and I spent most of the day stealing off to our private trailer. When we were shooting the part of the finale that featured you singing "Xanadu," I couldn't help but believe you were, once again, my own personal muse, singing right to me.

"And now, open your eyes and see what we have made is real. . . . "

Indeed, Livvy. We did it. You and Matt; me and Ann. And, for me, in only eleven days, right on schedule! That night I convinced Ann to join me at Fiorucci, where my old friend Greg, now an established clothing designer, was having a fashion show. Our first date in public. Dozens of stars, models, and paparazzi swarmed under the hot lights as a live DJ played pounding music. Ann ran into someone she knew and hugged the attractive girl whose green eyes were even more intense than hers, if that's possible. Then Ann said to me, "This is Danielle, she manages Fiorucci. Danielle, this is Betty . . . well, Hillary."

"Don't ask," I smiled.

"Don't need to," Danielle joked. "She's always up to something. I know that."

Then I remembered. Danielle was the one who had left my juggler friend Nick to be with Ann a couple of years ago. Sure Ann had a girlfriend now, but because I'd never met the "other woman," she didn't seem real. Danielle was there in the flesh, and it was hard not to feel jealous seeing Ann with an ex, especially one so charming.

At midnight when I dropped Ann off and we kissed good-bye in my car, I was busy wondering if and when we would kiss again. And if we'd ever get a chance to do more than just that.

The next evening Daisy returned from San Francisco, and I decided to cook dinner for her, which I never did because my cooking sucks. When she walked through the door, smelled curry and saffron, and saw the candlelit table, she burst into tears. This was something Daisy did about as often as I cooked.

"What's going on, Honey?" I asked. "Talk to me."

Between sobs she pushed out short sentences. "So much easier up there." "Too hard here." "Not good for us." "I'm moving back."

I started crying, too.

What had we done? This was two weeks before Christmas, the end of a decade, and change was slapping us both in the face.

Luckily Christmastime was one of the busiest times of the year for me since I also had a job delivering singing telegrams. Day and night I was racing around town as a singing, tap-dancing fruitcake with little time to think about Daisy, who was leaving after New Year's, or about Ann, who I hadn't seen nor heard a peep from since that night at Fiorucci, a whole week earlier. I'd lie awake late at night and wonder. If this thing with Ann was really "magic," why'd I feel so damn shitty?

Then one ominously cloudy Thursday morning a letter arrived in the mail. On a sixties greeting card it read: "We must meet for cocktails soon to discuss these anxieties I have. Somewhere discreet. The press is on to us." The card was signed "Ann," and was covered with lipstick kisses. At the bottom, in tiny print, she'd written: "It's better with Betty."

I was a goner.

"Is the enclosed discreet enough?" I wrote back, including an ad for a restaurant on a quiet Malibu beach. "No one will ever find us there. Be on the southeast corner at 4:00 p.m. Monday. Wear dark glasses and carry a white object."

That Monday in Malibu, Ann and I sipped fruity cocktails decorated with parasols and maraschino cherries and watched the cloud-obscured sun set over the ocean. We held hands under the table and said very little.

We drove to her house and it began to pour. We listened to Brian Eno's *Music for Airports* and couldn't keep our hands off each other. It's just so different with women rather than men, Livvy. Curves instead of angles, flesh instead of muscle, excitement building into a soft won't-you-come-in rather than a hard how-do-you-do.

Hillary Carlip

Ann asked me to stay that night. I had never wanted anything so badly, but I didn't want to throw it all in Daisy's face, so at 2:00 a.m. I drove home. By the time I arrived Daisy was so angry anyway, she chased me around the house with a hammer. I survived, unbludgeoned, but needless to say, we slept in separate beds.

The next day, for the first time ever in a relationship, I lied. I know, I know. I hated doing it, Livvy. But how many times had Daisy lied to me? I'd lost count.

We were in the kitchen, the hammer safely in the toolbox. We both had dark circles under our eyes. "I'm working late tonight—and I have an early telegram tomorrow all the way on the West Side," I told her. "So I'm gonna stay at my parents' house."

"Fine," she said. She seemed to believe me.

"Besides," I added, "we obviously need some space." At least that part was true.

I drove to Ann's. At long last we climbed into her bed together. Our touch was electrical, alchemical. I lost all sense of time and place, aware only of skin on skin, moving and melding into one body awash in the currents of espionage.

From that night on, every journal entry I wrote began with "OH MY."

The week between Christmas and New Year's was confusing. I slept at Ann's a few more times. Daisy and I spent New Year's Eve together, mostly crying and saying good-bye to the decade, and to all we had gone through together in it.

Three days later I drove Daisy to the Burbank Airport, where, under the late afternoon shade of palm trees, warmed by a balmy winter wind, we said our last good-byes.

I drove home, climbed into bed, and cried myself to sleep. I awoke the next morning with my heart still aching, but also with a tinge of excitement over the newness that was about to unfold. But I had to be patient. Ann was about to leave for a two-week trip *with her girlfriend.*

That night I drove to her place and handed her a going-away package. It included a bottle of invisible ink for her to write me secret letters with—"I'll keep the activator pen"; several love notes written on magician's flash paper—"They go up in smoke after you read them"; and a stamped metal token I'd made for her at the Santa Monica Pier. It read "Ann + Betty."

She then, totally unexpectedly, surprised me with a package of her own.

My hands were shaking as I opened it. Inside I found pink stationery embossed in gold lettering that read: "Better Believe It from Betty," a red fur pen with raspberry-scented ink, and—most exciting—a toothbrush, which I was instructed to leave at her house. We shared another passionate night and in the morning, neither of us wanted to let go.

The next week with Ann gone, I felt lost. I'd been working fourteen-hour days on the *Xanadu* shoot, delivering singing telegrams day and night, and spending time with two lovers. Now I was suddenly faced with little work, no lover near, and for the first time in my life, I was living alone. I eagerly waited for the mailman, who arrived every day empty-handed. Everything I read made me think of Ann—like *The Diary of Anaïs Nin*: "All unfulfilled desires are imprisoned children." Every song I heard reminded me of her—especially Rickie Lee Jones singing, "I will miss your company."

The following week the mailman finally appeared—an oasis in my Hollywood Hills desert—with letters. Every day. Ann wrote on stationery that was the same style of the "Better Believe It from Betty" paper, but embossed in gold on the top of hers was "Ann's-xieties." I was deliriously happy reading of her cabin fever and of how much she missed me. And even though she said she was confused and worried, she still signed all her letters with lines like, "I can't wait to see you," "Your Ann," and "Freezing in snow and burning for you."

I was at the top of the roller coaster, feeling exhilarated, but still prepared for the free fall that comes after those highs—so far they'd been a feature of life with Ann. But the fall would have to wait. Ann returned home with great news. She had told her girlfriend about me, and they'd finally broken up.

We spent the next two glorious weeks together. Even when we were out and she drank enough to let loose that nasty, bitter side, she was still the most exciting person I had ever been with. One night we decided to meet at a club, both in complete disguise, and "pick each other up." Another night we went to the Queen Mary—not the boat, but the female impersonator club. And each night we ended up in my bed or hers.

Then came the *Xanadu* wrap party at Flippers Roller Rink (where you looked fabulous, per usual, Livvy!). Ann said she'd meet me there. I nearly choked on a "disco cheese ball" when she walked in . . . *with her supposed ex-girlfriend*!

I'll tell you, Livvy, meeting the "other woman" face-to-face did me in. I wasn't messing with a concept—I saw a human being. One that I'm sure I'd been hurting. It totally freaked me out.

The next morning I called Ann and told her that if she was still seeing her girlfriend, we were through. By nighttime she showed up at my door, swearing she and the girl had broken up, for real. She had just taken her to the wrap party, she explained, because she felt guilty. Ann whisked me away to the Pickwick Drive-In movie theater. I have no idea what film was playing. Let's just say we didn't watch much.

Later that week I picked up a *Hollywood Reporter* and read that a major network was looking to cast regulars for a variety show: "Dancers who can swim needed to perform synchronized swimming routines."

I dared Ann to audition. She did. And she landed the job. Little did I know her rehearsal schedule would require her to wake up at 3:30 every morning, which took away a few more hours of our coveted time together.

The night before Valentine's Day, Ann came to my house to sleep over. After a beautiful evening together, she informed me that she had to spend the next day with her "ex." "I'm just trying to be nice to her," she explained.

"On Valentine's Day? Isn't that maybe sending her a mixed message?"

I wasn't sure if I could take any more of this, but I still gave her an art piece/valentine I had spent the previous week making for her. She loved it, but she had nothing for me except a sweet thank-you kiss that turned into more. When I woke at 6:00 a.m. on Valentine's Day, Ann was gone.

Stuffing my disappointment into my Cupid costume, I prepared for my busy day—delivering a record-breaking twenty-eight singing/ tap-dancing telegrams. Just as I was about to walk out the front door, I spotted something on the living room table. Piled high were gifts from Ann, each one wrapped in red paper with tiny white hearts. As torn as I had been, I once again fell completely and deeply. Not so much because of the brilliant gifts, oh, and they all were, but because Ann had waited without a word and surprised me so.

Over the next month Ann was as unpredictable as ever, and I was growing more and more nauseous riding the roller coaster with her. Still, whatever reservations I had always melted with her touch.

"Betty," she said one night as we sat down in my living room to watch the premiere of her variety show, "I've just felt so guilty this whole time."

I braced myself.

"I've decided to try and make it work with my girlfriend. I don't think I can see you anymore."

I was no longer on the roller coaster, Livvy. I was now on the Tilt-A-Whirl, hanging on for dear life. After dropping the bomb, she left my house with only a hug good-bye—a kiss would have been too risky for us both. And that was that.

For the next few weeks all I could do was weep and ponder what I had done. Was it right to end my three-year relationship for what now seemed like just a fantasy? Did I really think I'd end up being in a long-term relationship with someone where we didn't even call each other by our real names? And what is magic anyway? Even if it is up to us to believe in and manifest what we want, is what happens *after* that in our hands? Obviously, once we attain our desires, there are no guarantees. And maybe most of the time we don't even *know* what our *true* desires are. I guess all we can do is put one foot in front of the other and let destiny reveal itself.

Ready for this, Livvy?

Less than two months later, my clothing designer friend Greg calls and cries excitedly, "Dolllllll, I totally met someone for you today. I was buying shoes and put them on hold so you'll come back with me tomorrow and meet her."

"Where?" I ask.

"Fiorucci. She's the manager."

"Wait, you mean Danielle?"

"Yes."

That's right, Livvy. Danielle. The juggler's ex. Ann's old ex.

Then, that very night, before I'd even gone with Greg to Fiorucci, which we'd arranged to do the next day, I go to Peanuts (a women's club you might have heard of, Liv—just in case the rumors about you ARE true!). I walk in, and there, standing at the bar as if divinely choreographed in a routine way more impressive than any in *Xanadu,* is a charming girl with intense green eyes who looks awfully familiar.

"Who's that?" I ask a friend.

"Her name's Danielle."

I say hello, and within minutes we're joking, laughing, talking as if we've known each other forever. And that's the night that Danielle and I begin a relationship that's still going strong today, almost a year later.

So you're right, Livvy. You do have to believe in magic. And if all your hopes survive—destiny *will* arrive.

We can never be certain what magic looks like, but thanks to you, Livvy, I'm a believer.

Love,

Hillary Carlip

P.S. I'm sorry the *London Evening News* said *Xanadu* was "the most dreadful, tasteless movie of all time" and *Los Angeles* magazine described your acting as "having the range of a mannequin." Despite the bad reviews, I hope you continue to believe in magic!

SHOOTING CALL
UNIVERSAL CITY STUDIOS, INC.
Due to Extreme Fire Hazard, Please Be Careful Smoking. Use Butt Cans.

Picture				Unit 13ᵗʰ	Day of Shooting
XANADU					

Series		No. 02130	Director Robert Greenwald

Art Director John Corso	Date THURSDAY Oct 4, 1979
Set Dresser Mara Meyer	Shooting Call Time 7:00 A / Condition of Call
	☒ PA CREW / REPORT TO LOCATION ☐ BUS TO LOCATION

SET DESCRIPTION	SC. NO.	D/N	LOCATION
Int - Fiorucci at Ramp (Kira, Danny, Sonny, Atmos) — skate down Rampland into dressing room	112	N	Fiorucci 206 N. Rodeo Dr Beverly Hills Ca
Int - Fiorucci Line of Dressing Rooms (Atmos) — Chorus line comes out with spider man	113	N	

1

118   INT. XANADU   NIGHT

Kira and Sonny dancing. twiling as before in Fiorucci.
They stop and look at each other. There's no mistaking
the look between them.

In a booth nearby is Danny and Richie. Danny's talking on
the telephone. Richie's looking at Kira and Sonny ~~and~~ just
slightly ~~~~ whistfully.

                    RICHIE
          I wonder what would hve happened
          if I got that album to paint.

                    DANNY
             (into phone)
          Yeah, ~~~~ that's right, we're
          opening tomorrow night...well you
          can bring your tv cameras if you
          want but we're not doing all that
          celebrity stuff..nope, just people..anyone
          ~~~~ who shows up..eight o'clock,
          right. See you tomorrow.

He hangs up the phone. Speaks to Richie who's still
looking at Sonny and Kira.

Fall
1980

❊ I'm unable to audition for more movies, since the Screen Actor's Guild goes on strike. Less than two weeks after the strike ends, former SAG president Ronald Reagan is elected president of the United States.

❊ Three hundred fifty million viewers tune in to find out "Who Shot J.R." A month later, we learn that Mark David Chapman, a deranged fan, shot, and killed, John Lennon.

❊ I use a whole sheet of legal paper to make a note to remind myself to try the newly released product by 3M—Post-its.

❊ CNN launches the first all-news network, just in time to watch the U.S.-supported Iraqi president, Saddam Hussein, invade and attack Iran.

❊ I see a new band called the Go-Go's perform in small clubs as they try to get a record deal.

* A fire at the MGM Grand Hotel in Las Vegas kills eighty-four people, and Toxic Shock Syndrome claims the lives of thirty-eight women. The hit TV show *Happy Days* is in its sixth season.

* Danielle's roommate, a gay twenty-year-old named Freddie, is very sick with a suppressed immune system, yet no doctor can figure out a diagnosis for him.

* Fifteen-year-old Brooke Shields seductively whispers in a commercial, "Nothing comes between me and my Calvins." The ad is banned.

* I hang out with my new "buddy," Kristy McNichol, whose show, *Family,* goes off the air.

Me (in costume) with Kristy

Jack Haley Jr.'s Coat Closet

On a breezy, mesquite-scented autumn night, I pull up to Jack Haley Jr.'s lavish West Hollywood home in the hills north of Sunset Boulevard. The parking valet, a young Latino in a pink vest, pink bow tie, and pink cap, whisks open my door.

"I'll only be ten or fifteen minutes," I tell him. "Can I just leave my car in front?"

"No problemo, but if it's longer, I have to move it."

"It won't be."

I step out of the car, and when the valet catches sight of my ensemble—gold-trimmed black cancan dress encrusted with sequins, black fishnet stockings, gold lamé gloves, and a large black feather rising from the side of a jeweled headband—he lets loose a big, cartoony wolf whistle.

"Ay, *Mamacita*! And I thought *my* work getup was out there!"

"You look good in pink," I tease as I reach into the backseat and retrieve my concertina—a kind of miniature accordion—and a basket filled with a long loaf of French bread, a round of cheese, and an apple.

I balance on shiny spiked heels, walking up the red brick driveway, its cracks grouted with grass. When I miss a brick, my heel squishes deep into moist, dewy green. Noise spills from inside the house like a soundtrack to a party—glasses clinking, guests chatting—reminding me of the cocktail parties I'd hear from my childhood bedroom and smell on my mother's breath when she later tucked me in.

I gather my nerve, ring the doorbell, and wait.

A slender, blond man wearing a paisley ascot opens the door. "Shit, you're early," he whispers theatrically as he grabs my arm and whisks me down the hallway, careful to make sure no one sees me.

"It's ten o'clock, I'm right on time," I whisper back.

"Well, we're not ready yet, come on." He leads me to a door. I assume the door opens to a den where I will wait, stealing a glimpse of framed photographs from Jack Haley Jr.'s life—him sitting in a director's chair on the set of his hit film, *That's Entertainment*; with Liza Minelli on exotic vacations during their five-year marriage; his dad as the Tin Man on the set of *The Wizard of Oz*.

But no. *I'm taken into a coat closet.* The man closes the door behind us both. He's pressed up against me in the small, dark space, and I can smell vodka on his breath and mousse in his hair.

"Sorry, but everything started late," he says. "We had a disaster in the kitchen. If you'll just wait here a bit, I'll make it worth your while." I feel him fishing for something in his pocket, and then a flame appears, hissing from a gold lighter. It illuminates the twenty-dollar bill he holds.

"I guess I can wait a bit."

"Thanks a lot." He hands me the twenty dollars and slips out, quickly shutting the door behind him. I hear a man in the hallway say loudly, clearly for the benefit of the other guests, "Well, Mark, it's about time you came out of the closet!" Partygoers laugh.

I put down my basket and concertina and lean against the cologne-scented jackets and perfumed-tinged furs. In the three years since I began delivering singing telegrams, I've experienced many odd situations, but hiding in a coat closet is a first. While almost all deliveries go smoothly and on time, I have discovered that when I'm made to wait, it's usually for a delivery to a celebrity. And working in the heart of Hollywood for Live Wires Singing Telegram Company, I've had my share of celebrity recipients.

Tonight David Niven Jr. has sent me to celebrate a double birthday for Jack Haley Jr. and star of stage and screen Tony *"The Name of the Game"* Franciosa. Like his friend Jack, Tony had married and divorced a legendary actress—in his case, Shelley Winters. When I get out of this closet, I will perform my most popular telegram, the "fabulous, fantastic, fiery, frenzied, famous Fifi DeLune," a sequined French cancan girl who delivers comedy patter while she juggles, sings a song appropriate for the occasion, then leaves the recipient with a mini French feast, which she also juggles.

When delivering singing telegrams I mostly perform my own characters and original material: a fortune-telling gypsy, a nagging wife, a Salvation Army zealot sent to cocktail parties to encourage the recipient to "repent," a scheming Lucille Ball, a stewardess taking recipients on a "trip" through their lives, a nagging Jewish mother, and a porn director who comically leads the fully-clothed recipient in scenes from their "latest film." I also do specific holiday characters created by Live Wires: a leprechaun for St. Patrick's Day, a fruitcake for Christmas, a baby for Mother's Day.

I know it's not like performing on television or in films, but at least I'm not waitressing while I wait for my big break. And since I often perform for studio heads, producers, casting directors, and stars, I figure delivering singing telegrams could very well lead to something bigger. Jack Haley Jr. is a successful producer, and who knows who else is at this party. So I guess it's worth the wait. Even in this closet.

After ten minutes, I hear footsteps approaching. *Finally.* I adjust my strapless bra, make sure the feather in my headband's standing straight. I pick up my basket and concertina. I'm ready. The knob turns, and Mark opens the door a crack. He pokes his head in and whispers, "Just a little bit longer. Can I get you a drink?"

"No thanks," I say, sucking in the fresh air that seeps through the gap. "But I do have to get going soon," I add as the door closes.

Damn it. Just last week I stood for twenty minutes on the corner of Rodeo Drive and Santa Monica Boulevard in front of the Beverly Hills Presbyterian Church dressed as a gorilla. When I was finally led into the church, I sang, danced, and told gorilla-themed jokes for a famous movie star. I really shouldn't say her name because, well, *I was appearing at her Alcoholics Anonymous meeting,* sent to celebrate her two-year anniversary of "having the gorilla off her back."

And a few weeks before that I waited thirty minutes dressed as a fifties-style fan in the back of a soundstage at Paramount Studios as they taped the first episode of the fourth season of *Laverne and Shirley* in front of a live studio audience. Penny Marshall and Cindy Williams had hired me and my cohort to welcome back the cast, whom we thought we were waiting to greet backstage when the scene was over. Wrong. After a half hour, a producer ran up to us and, without warning, shooed us out onto the stage, where we unexpectedly performed our routine for the entire cast, crew, and studio audience.

At least during those two incidents, I could breathe. It's getting pretty damn stuffy in this closet. And I do have a life. In fact, I have a date with Danielle. I'm supposed to meet her at a club at 10:30. That's in ten minutes. Come on already.

Finally the door opens. A wrinkled blond woman in her seventies wearing a silver cocktail dress, jumps back. "What the fuck?!" she yelps.

"Shhhh," I whisper, "I'm a surprise for the birthday boys."

"Ya nearly gave me a motherfuckin' heart attack." She is so sloshed, she stumbles inside the closet, and I manage to catch her by the arm before she falls.

"Can I help you with something?"

"My lipschhhtick," she slurs, rummaging through the coats. "I left it in my pocket." This woman can barely stand up straight. How the hell is she going to apply lipstick? Still, I help her search and I find the cool, smooth tube in a leather coat pocket.

"Thanksssss," she says as I hand it to her. She staggers out, closing the door on me.

Hillary Carlip

One time I was sent to Chasen's restaurant to deliver a singing telegram for Ed McMahon's birthday. Not only did I have to wait twenty minutes until his guests finished their appetizers, but once I finally started performing, Ed *heckled* me. I improvised as best I could, working around his obnoxious comments, but he was relentless. Finally one of his guests, the typically even *more* obnoxious Don Rickles, came to my rescue, shouting, "Ed, shut up and listen!"

Months earlier, at a party in Coldwater Canyon, I waited for Steve Allen to stop noodling on the piano before I could begin my act. When he didn't, I dived into my routine anyway, and he kept playing, trying to accompany me. At least I made the guests laugh when, in character, I asked him to please stop. "I work alone," I said.

And alone I wait, for another fifteen minutes, in Jack Haley Jr.'s coat closet. Trying to remain cool, I mentally recite a litany of Zen quotes that I recall: "If you understand, things are just as they are; if you do not understand, things are just as they are." "The obstacle is the path." Insightful, but not really relevant to having to wait in a friggin' closet.

Finally I hear footsteps. But it sounds like the click of high heels. Again the door opens a crack and this time a buxom caterer dressed in a short black skirt and crisp white hors d'oeuvre-stained shirt thrusts a tray inside. "Potsticker?"

I decline. "Would you mind telling Mark I have to go?"

"Who?"

"The guy in the paisley ascot."

"Which one?"

Figures. I describe Mark's particular paisley, and she ventures out to find him. Now my future lies in the hands of a stranger whose priority is to deliver rounds of crab cakes. It's 10:35, and I'm already five minutes late to meet Danielle, and I haven't even performed yet. And it's not like I'm getting paid by the hour. I get a set fee for what usually takes ten minutes, and I've been here thirty-five minutes already. Who do these people think they are, anyway? Just because they've had some success doesn't mean they can treat others like they're unimportant. It's always the celebrities. . . .

I remember one chilly spring day when I arrived at a lavish estate tucked into Benedict Canyon. I rang the bell, and the large wooden front doors creaked open. There stood Cher. Even dressed in baggy gray sweatpants, a T-shirt, and no makeup, she was striking.

"Come in," she said excitedly. "I'll go get Chas." She didn't move—just screamed upstairs. "Chas, come on down, someone's here for you."

In the foyer, assorted kids and adults gathered around me. Cher called upstairs a few more times, but when her daughter, Chastity, didn't answer, one of the guests, a very tan woman, climbed the stairs.

Cher talked with her guests while I waited. And waited. Finally, about fifteen minutes later, the tan woman appeared at the top of the stairs with Cher's eleven-year-old daughter. The birthday girl sauntered downstairs, and I launched into my routine. Everyone laughed and applauded. Except for Chastity, who never cracked a smile.

As I was leaving, Cher turned to the apathetic birthday girl, "Chas? What do you say?"

"Thank you," her daughter uttered, almost inaudibly.

Not quite the enthusiastic response one would desire after being made to wait.

At this point even a standing ovation won't make forty-five minutes in this closet worthwhile. I hear everyone singing "Happy Birthday," and I feel my lip curling. Okay, I have to draw the line somewhere. How can they be so thoughtless and rude? They think it's okay to make me wait this long in a dark, tiny coat closet like freakin' Patty Hearst? Unh-unh. Enough already. My heart's pounding, muffled under my lace bra; my palms are damp with sweat in my gold lamé gloves. I can hardly breathe. That's it, I'm outta here.

Just as I reach for the doorknob, I feel it turn. Mark pokes his head in. "Pllleeeeaaassse forgive me. I am sooooo sorry. It's just that everyone was still doing dinner, and I knew they wouldn't focus while they ate, and I just want this to be perfect. We're finishing up cake right now and I swear it'll only be five more minutes. I swear."

"Look, it's been almost an hour, and I'm already late for my next appointment." I try to appear cool, to keep my anger from erupting. He could be an important showbiz connection. But I take a stand and say, "I have to go now."

"I'll make it worth your while," he repeats, only this time he reaches into his pocket and takes out *two* twenty-dollar bills. Damn. What do I do? I need the money for rent this month. I only make twenty-five bucks for delivering the singing telegram, and usually people don't even tip. I can't say no to forty more dollars, can I?

"All right," I hiss, snatching the bills. "But if it's not in five minutes, I'm gone."

"Thank you so much!" Mark hugs me. I feel his silk ascot brush against my cleavage; some mousse from his hair sticks to my left cheek. The door closes, and once again I'm enfolded in darkness.

I am still so riled, my heart won't stop racing. There are a million things I want to do with my life yet I spend so much time waiting. Waiting in lines at the bank and post office, in traffic, and for buses. Waiting for phone calls from lovers, for food to come at restaurants, for planes to take off, for news that I got the job. I've waited to say the right thing at the right time, waited for apologies, and waited until the last minute to make a decision. I've spent an enormous portion of my life waiting. And what have I done with that time? Grown impatient, antsy, annoyed, insulted, angry, frustrated, exasperated.

And right there in Jack Haley Jr.'s coat closet, it hits me—just how much energy I've wasted. I breathe deeply and calm myself down as I make a decision. I will no longer continue to waste my life while I wait. Instead, I'll use my time and materials wisely. I will brainstorm and scheme, meditate, contemplate, create. Damn it, from now on, while I wait, I might even enjoy myself. After all, I do have a choice.

Before I can put my newfound revelation into practice, the door opens, light pours in, and Mark says, "You're on!"

I place my basket back on my arm, pick up my concertina, and pull out its folds, sucking in air. I launch into the cancan song as I march into the living room. Forty guests, all decked out in cocktail dresses and suits, are gathered in the stark, white room with white furniture and white shag carpeting. They gasp and giggle as I enter, and when I finish my song on the concertina, they applaud.

"Sank you," I say in a thick French accent. "Sank you. In English, how you say *Thank you*." The partygoers laugh. I'm off to a good start.

"My name is Fifi DeLune and I am looking for zee birthday boys, Jacques and Tony. Where are you?"

Liza Minnelli and Shelley Winters's ex-husbands sheepishly raise their hands while their friends point them out. As I perform, the audience stays completely with me. For my finale, I reach into my basket and pull out the long loaf of French bread, the round of Edam cheese, and the apple. I juggle the feast and each time the apple passes my mouth in the pattern, I take bites of it. A real crowd-pleaser. As I finish my act, everyone hoots and hollers, claps and whistles.

The birthday boys approach me. "Great job," Jack says. "That was really something," Tony adds.

We're interrupted by guests coming up to say good-night to their hosts. I wave good-bye and move quickly toward the front door. In the hallway, a voice stops me.

"Fifi!"

I turn and see Mark. "It was perfect," he says as he hugs me again.

"Thanks," I say, and I head outside to the valet. I can tell I was the party's finale by the twelve people already standing in line for their cars. The valet in the matching pink vest, bow tie, and cap sees me and calls out, "Sorry, Mamacita, you took longer than fifteen minutes. I had to move your car."

I look at the line in front of me and smile. "No problem," I say. "I don't mind waiting."

Hillary Carlip

LIVE WIRES

The Singing Telegram People...By foot or by phone.

1983

* A decade after sweating on the picket line at anti-war demonstrations with Jane Fonda, I sweat with her in the aerobics classes she teaches at her Jane Fonda Workout studio.
* Danielle, my girlfriend of three years, moves in, and for the first time I consider a long-term, monogamous relationship. Meanwhile, in Arizona, a man has long-term, polygamous relationships with 105 wives.
* I go to AIDS marches while the CDC warns blood banks of a possible problem with the blood supply. There are 3,064 cases of AIDS reported in the United States this year, and President Reagan hasn't yet mentioned the word "AIDS" in public; he will not do so for two more years, when there are 15,948 cases and the death toll exceeds 8,000.
* Several friends of mine are diagnosed as HIV-positive or have contracted AIDS.
* Tom Cruise dances around in his underwear in *Risky Business* while Jennifer Beals's dance double dances around in her underwear in *Flashdance*.
* Jenny Craig launches and competes with other popular diets—Weight Watchers, Pritikin, the Beverly Hills Diet, and Herbalife

("Lose Weight Now, Ask Me How")—while thirty-two-year-old Karen Carpenter dies of anorexia nervosa.

* Every Thursday night, I gather with six friends for "Knots Night," where we all watch and comment on our fave show, *Knots Landing*.

* The Supreme Court reaffirms its *Roe v. Wade* right to abortion (even though the initial court decision was ten years ago), and Sally Ride becomes the first American woman sent into space (even though the Soviet Union sent a woman into space twenty years ago).

* While I am cast in several films in various "Punk Girl" roles, my parents throw a punk party, and all their suburban friends show up in costume. Dinner is served when a construction site Roach Coach rolls up my parents' driveway and "caters" the event.

Anyone Can Be a Rock Star, or How to Be an Imposter

1. Begin by continually judging yourself, disliking particular qualities you possess or, more accurately, lack.
2. Pick a character—any persona—who is imbued with traits you desire.
3. Shrouded in anonymity—an alter ego who is tougher, wiser, more gregarious than you are—know you *cannot* fail. If you do, it is not you failing but someone with another name, another history, another style, another life.
4. Try on "Angel," a tough-talking, gum-chomping ex-con who served time in the slammer for offenses you never reveal. Simply assure people, "It wasn't murder or nuthin'."
5. Create your new history—with details of your time served and how you found the light behind bars—not in Jesus or the Bible, but in *TV reruns*.
6. Spread the "good word" of a return to simpler, more innocent times through music. Write songs about reruns—"Beaver Cleaver Fever," "Ode to Mrs. Kravitz," and your most controversial, "Buffy Come Back," a tribute to the sweet, freckled girl with blond pigtails from *Family Affair*. Anissa Jones, the actress

who portrayed the precocious child who went everywhere with her best friend, Mrs. Beasley, the nearsighted doll with square-framed glasses, died at the age of eighteen of a massive drug overdose at a friend's house in Oceanside, California. Write an anti-drug, cautionary tale with lyrics like:

> *Forget Buffy's drugs that go on and kill us*
> *Why not get high on Dobie Gillis?*
> *There's one other drug that won't make you puke*
> *You know I'm talking 'bout Patty Duke.*
> *Buffy, Buffy come back to me, why'd you have to go and OD,*
> *who will watch over Mrs. Beasley?*
> *Buffy, Buffy come back to me, why'd you have to go and OD,*
> *what about Uncle Bill, Jody, and Cissy?*

7. Ask a brilliant musician friend who has been in bands like Oingo Boingo to help you write the music to your songs and put together an "all-girl, all ex-con band."

8. Find a makeshift recording studio in Miracle Mile, above Ohrbach's department store. Make sure it's a small, windowless room painted cactus green, smelling of cigarettes and gardenia air freshener, and crammed with four-track recording equipment, which is almost as old as the saber-toothed tiger bones trapped in the La Brea Tar Pits one block east.

9. Meet your new band, some of the best female musicians and backup singers in town—one has played keyboards with Prince, another was in Fanny, one of the first seventies all-girl rock groups. Be impressed. Be grateful.

10. While the band sets up, rehearse with your new backup singers. Make it clear that you know your singing sucks, and you don't begin to think you can sound like they do. Observe as they create elaborate harmonies that are so tightly blended, for the first time you viscerally understand the word *harmonious*. Instantly

bond with your backup singers—joke, laugh, share stories, bare lives. Name them the Reruns. Feel like you belong.

11. Since you've never done anything like this before, as you're about to record your vocals, take several deep breaths and try to exhale enormous self-doubt. Jump up and down in place and fling your hands, allowing the nerves to shoot out of your fingertips onto Wilshire Boulevard. Remind yourself *it's Angel singing. Not you.* When you hear the band play the intro to the song, be so blown away that you forget your anxiety altogether.

12. Finish recording at 2:00 a.m. Shout, applaud, and laugh giddily with everyone as you all listen to both songs, "Buffy Come Back" and "Beaver Cleaver Fever."

13. Say to the band and to your girls, the Reruns, "No matter what it takes, I'm gonna get these songs out into the world."

14. Possessed with determination fueled by the safety net of your masquerade, spend the next six months learning and doing things you've never done before: (a) Go to the county recorder to establish a business for your record company; (b) Design graphics for the front and back of the record sleeve as well as the inside label, and get them printed; (c) Take your master tapes to a record plant and listen to countless test pressings on vinyl until the sound is perfectly captured on the black 45 rpm discs; (d) Pick up the finished singles packed in neat cardboard boxes, each stamped with blocky red letters: ANGEL AND THE RERUNS.

15. Do your research. Listen to KROQ, the number-one radio station in L.A., specifically to a show every Sunday night called "Rodney on the ROQ" that features new, alternative music. Find out everything you can about the host, Rodney Bingenheimer— how he was the first to interview and play songs by Blondie, Billy Idol, Duran Duran, the Sex Pistols, and countless other bands whose careers he's helped launch. Imagine yourself, or more accurately Angel, as his next discovery.

16. Dress in a multicolored, bouncy tulle skirt with a brown leather biker vest, bold lines of silver studs on the back spelling out ANGEL. At all times wear Ray-Ban sunglasses, framed by your eighties punk haircut—short on the sides, tall spikes on top. Draw a tattoo on your left arm that says "DAD" in a heart, a halo on your right arm, and your look is complete. Dress your girls, the Reruns, in exotic, patterned fifties sheath dresses and tease their wigs into overdone bouffant hairdos.

17. Drive over to the KROQ studios in Pasadena. Inhale the chilly January air that still smells like roses. After parking ask the Reruns in your tough-girl voice, "All right, we all ready to kick some ass?" Have the Reruns answer in unison, "Ready, Angel." Stick to your story that you all met in the slammer and continue your jailhouse dynamic out on the streets—you are their leader, their daddy; they acquiesce to you and do so in obedient synchronicity.

18. Knock on the back door of the studio. When a man with a blue mohawk answers, lie and say, "Rodney's expecting us." If you can convince Rodney to play "Buffy Come Back," tonight could be a huge break. But first you have to get in to see him.

19. With Angel's balls leading the way, push past the man at the door and, despite his protests, walk down the hall to the studio where a light flashes by a sign that reads "DO NOT ENTER WHEN RED LIGHT IS ON." Boldly push open the door. Have the girls run up to Rodney and kiss him all over his face, leaving red lip prints as souvenirs. Notice why Rodney, thin and boyish though well into his forties, was Davy Jones's stand-in on the TV show *The Monkees*. Observe his mop-top bowl haircut and tight, hip-hugging, pin-striped bell-bottoms with mod leather ankle boots. Watch as the girls' lipstick prints fade into the color his face turns when he blushes.

20. Say, "Hey, Rodney, we're Angel and the Reruns and we got somethin' for you" as you hand him your hot-off-the-presses record. Watch as Rodney puts on his large headphones, fades out the

record that's just ending, and talks into a microphone. "This is KROQ, Rodney on the ROQ, and some visitors just popped in that I want to introduce. What's your name again?" Answer "Angel and the Reruns" as you chomp on a piece of chewing gum. Keep cool as Rodney takes your 45 out of its sleeve, puts it on a turntable, and says, "They've brought us a new song and, well, they just look so great I'm gonna do something I rarely do. I'm gonna play their record without even listening to it first. What's the name of the song?" Lean into the microphone and say smoothly, "'Buffy Come Back.' Right girls?" "Right Angel."

21. As your song plays on the radio, observe Rodney leaning back in his chair and listening. Notice how he laughs everywhere he should and taps his foot along with the beat. When it's over and Rodney leans into the microphone to say, "That was fantastic. Angel and the Reruns in their radio debut. Great song. We'll be right back," wait until he hits a button and a commercial comes on before you and the girls shriek with excitement.

22. Don't overstay your welcome. Thank Rodney and head to the door. Stop in your tracks when the man with the blue mohawk bursts in, saying, "The phones are lighting up, man. Looks like everyone digs 'Buffy.'"

23. When Rodney asks you to stick around, shrug like you're a rock star, and say, "Yeah, okay. I guess we could stay a bit longer." When he then asks you to answer some phone calls on the air, keep up the ruse—especially when some of the callers are friends of yours, even your mother, pretending, as you previously planned, to be random listeners who freaked out over the song and are requesting to hear it again.

24. Three weeks later when "Buffy" has become the number-one re-quested song on KROQ, drive down Sunset Boulevard with your dog, Paisley, in the backseat. As you pass Laurel Canyon, where as a teenager you staked out Carole King, sing along with Eu-rythmics' "Sweet Dreams" on the radio. When you drive by the

Source restaurant, where every time you go for watermelon juice or brown rice pancakes you see some famous musician, start to feel lightheaded as you hear a familiar keyboard riff. Pull over to the side of the road when you suddenly hear your voice. *On the radio. In the middle of the day. On a station other than KROQ.* Scream, "WHOOO HOOOO!" as Paisley joins in, howling. Finally feel good about yourself. Well, feel good about Angel.

25. Over the next several months, as "Buffy Come Back" spreads to local stations, then national, and then international, becoming, as the DJs call it, a "cult hit," dive in even more deeply, taking the band to the next step: (a) Do a photo shoot, which results in a smoky black-and-white Avedon-like 8 x 10; (b) Write a press release, headline claiming: "JAILBIRDS TURN SONGBIRDS"; (c) Put together packets with the release, the photo, and the record; (d) Create another persona to be Angel's assistant—use a fake name you've used in your past and, as Madelyn Evans, call newspapers and magazines to hype the story of the band; (e) Send out packets to media; (f) Answer the phone that rings endlessly; (g) Write more songs and rehearse with the band; (h) Drive from store to store distributing the records out of the trunk of your car.

26. Drink lots of coffee and find good under-eye concealer to hide the dark circles.

27. Do interviews with the newspapers and magazines who respond to your packets; then, once they are published, excitedly read the pieces that say things like: *"Move over Go-Go's. Los Angeles seems to be the perfect spawning ground for all-girl groups who have a tendency to bullet to the top. . . . As long as the group can stay on the good side of the law for a while, it looks like it's hitsville for Angel and the Reruns, L.A.'s bad girls gone good."*

28. Book the band on television shows—Alan Thicke's *Thicke of the Night* and a daytime show featuring Leslie Uggams called *Fantasy.* Perform twice on *Dance Fever* with guest judges from your

favorite reruns, including Lumpy, June Cleaver, and the Beave himself from *Leave It to Beaver*, who are all appreciative of your exaltation.

29. Spend a month shooting the film *Bachelor Party* and hang out with the up-and-coming star of the film, Tom Hanks.

30. Get one of your songs into the movie *Grandview, U.S.A.*, starring Jamie Lee Curtis and Patrick Swayze.

31. Do *everything* on your own. Explaining to someone else how to do things rather than just doing them yourself takes too long, and you can't be sure they will be done correctly. So as Angel and the Reruns get increasing attention and opportunities, discover your energy waning. Be careful not to careen toward total exhaustion and burnout.

32. Decide it's time to perform live: (a) Look for a club; (b) Book the club; (c) Rehearse even more; (d) Design flyers; (e) Distribute flyers; (f) Do sound checks; (g) Have "Madelyn Evans" call local news stations and build up hype.

33. On opening night, do interviews with CBS, ABC, and NBC news, as well as several magazines and newspapers.

34. During the run, continue doing your best—not just for the sold-out audience, but also for the reviewers in the house.

35. Excitedly await a specific review in the important music magazine that could catapult your career. When the issue hits the stands, buy up all the copies.

36. Go home and sit on the couch with Paisley while you read the review. Smile with satisfaction when you read: *"Refreshing concept . . . impressive chops . . . solid talent."*

37. Suddenly feel the loss of breath and sting of tears when you get to the end of the review.

38. Read it again, just to make sure you read it correctly the first time. *"This group—minus Angel—can be charming. It seemed the only one who couldn't sing (or act) was Angel herself."*

39. Sit very still, stunned. Try to figure out what to do with these

devastating barbs. If the reviewer is saying Angel can't sing that's one thing. But to say she can't *act*. . . . Angel's not acting. You're acting as Angel. It's a direct slam to you, and that's why you chose to hide behind Angel to begin with—to avoid the kind of harsh judgment from others that you already heap upon yourself.

40. Try to catch your breath, which is, indeed, eluding your chase. For days your lungs feel like a dirt-filled vacuum bag. When you finally go to the doctor and find out you have a serious respiratory infection and have to stay in bed for at least a week, you're not sure whether you're pissed off or grateful.

41. While confined to your bed, drinking teas of licorice root and eucalyptus, meditate, ponder, analyze, dissect. Look through old journals of yours as you try to discover/uncover what led you to this point. Reclaim your history.

42. Stumble upon a quote that moved you enough to include in your journal ten years earlier, though you have no memory of writing it there. Read the quote, by Joseph Chaiken from his book, *The Presence of the Actor*. *"In former times acting meant simply putting on a disguise. When you took off the disguise, there was the old face under it. Now it's clear that the wearing of the disguise changes the person. As he takes the disguise off, his face is changed from having worn it."*

43. Know that, thanks to Angel, your face has indeed changed and decide it's time to take off your disguise.

44. As weeks and months pass and your deeply ingrained insecurities and judgments start to creep back to the surface, oil on water, realize it's once again getting harder and harder to look at your own face in the mirror.

45. See #2.

Hillary Carlip

1985

✳ I take on another persona—Mindy Greenfield, co-creator of Cindy and Mindy's Rent-A-Fan Club. We get loads of press, and everyone, including *People* magazine, thinks I'm really Mindy Greenfield.

WORK IS A SCREAM FOR L.A.'S LISSA NEGRIN AND MINDY GREENFIELD, WHO ARE EXPERTS IN FAN-FLARE

✳ Go on the game show *Sale of the Century*, which I'm really good at when I watch at home. Except when taping the show, I suck. Luckily no one knows it's me sucking because I appear as Mindy Greenfield—wig and all. (P.S. Mindy won a crystal punch bowl set.)

✻ Vera, one more alias I assume, gets her own show, *Confidentially, Vera*, on KCET, local public television.

✻ New York City drug dealers introduce crack cocaine to the streets, while Whitney Houston scores her first hit with "You Give Good Love."

✻ Coke changes its original formula and introduces "New Coke."

✻ I move into a 1910 Craftsman house with my manager, Sam, and his boyfriend, Ken. We lease-to-own, and in a matter of months we're able to buy the house with money we make from renting it out as a location for film and TV shoots. Sylvester Stallone hawks ham in our living room, Keith Carradine is thrown through the glass of our porch window, and snow falls in our kitchen.

✻ Sam and I create a TV show called "It's a Miracle," which features true stories. Every network we pitch it to passes, saying "No one watches reality shows."

✻ My brother meets the woman who will become his wife and the mother of his two children.

✻ I study the "Course in Miracles" with Marianne Williamson, am rebirthed underwater in a bathtub, perspire heavily in an hour-long Native American sweat lodge ritual, and take "Making Relationships Work" classes with Rev. Terry Cole-Whittaker.

The Case of the Inexplicable Birthday Treasure Hunt

Despite my parents' desperate attempts to break me from the habit, I've always had to sleep with a light on. When I'm sleeping with someone, then I'm okay turning it off, but not when I'm alone. This is probably one of the reasons I am a serial monogamist.

After my five-year relationship with Danielle ends—and she runs off to be with someone else *the day after we break up*—not much more than a month passes before I start seeing Nora. Two women together tend to become family—sisters, mothers, daughters, partners, best friends—so there is rarely a breakup that is clean. And my relationship with Danielle is no exception. Five months later we still desperately miss each other, weep on the phone when we speak, spend much of our time together, and she even sleeps over at my new house, though I won't go near her new apartment, where she spends time with the "other" woman who I kindly refer to as "that bitch with the mole."

I have been clear with Nora from the start, letting her know that I just want to date—my heart still broken, I'm in no position to be in any kind of committed relationship. And she doesn't seem to mind, or at least she says she doesn't.

Most of the time I feel confused, torn, and drained.

So when the phone wakes me at 8:00 a.m. on the day before my twenty-ninth birthday, I am annoyed that I have to start another listless day so early. I turn off the vintage cowboy lamp by my bed and answer.

"Is this Hillary?" a woman's voice asks.

"Yes, who's this?" I mutter.

"I'm calling to let you know you must pick up a package waiting at the Bullocks department store gift-wrapping counter at exactly four p.m. today. Ask for Mrs. Blanchford, and say the word *pistachio*."

"What?"

"Four o'clock. Exactly."

"Who's the package from?"

"I'm not at liberty to say," the anonymous voice replies before swiftly hanging up.

Ever since my Girl from U.N.C.L.E. days I've remained a devout sleuth. Over the years, even well into my twenties, I have read and reread *Harriet the Spy* countless times, and solved every case in the *Encyclopedia Brown* boy detective books, cheating and peeking at the solutions in the back just once or twice, and only for the most complicated whodunits like "The Case of the Mysterious Tramp."

Any good detective would shudder with excitement receiving a phone call like the one from Mrs. Blanchford. But not me. Not now. These days it takes everything in me just to drag my ass from the living room to the kitchen to retrieve a butterscotch Jell-O Pudding Pop.

For the rest of the day I use most of my energy avoiding work and debating whether or not the trip to Bullocks at "four o'clock exactly" is worth the effort. The only thing that finally propels me to climb in my car and drive to the department store is the thought that whatever awaits me might be from Danielle.

I arrive at the third-floor gift-wrapping section six minutes before the appointed time. An elderly, well-groomed man working behind the counter is the only person in sight.

"Is Mrs. Blanchford here, please?" I ask.

"Sorry Ma'am." He looks up from curling a lavender ribbon with a scissors. "No one by that name works here."

"Are you sure? A Mrs. Blanchford called me at the crack of dawn this morning. She said you were holding a package for me. Oh. . . ." I suddenly remember. "PISTACHIO."

"Ah," he lays down his scissors. "You must be Hillary."

He slips into the back and returns a few seconds later carrying a box. I look up at the board of samples above his head and note that my mystery sender opted for Gift Wrap C, the paper with a treasure map motif.

"Can you please tell me who this is from?"

"Sorry, my shift just began," he says. "I haven't a clue."

I thank him and head to the ladies room. I've never been very good at receiving—much more comfortable giving. Whenever I've had a birthday party, I've insisted that no one bring gifts, and if people ignored my request, I couldn't bear to open presents in front of them. I'd wait until they left and then send a note later: "Love the pixie salt and pepper shakers, thanks a mill!"

I know I will have privacy inside the ladies lounge. I walk onto a floor of tiny brown and beige tiles neatly arranged like candies in a sampler box. I sit down in a folding chair and tear open the package to find a white terrycloth robe so plush, just holding it in my lap is comforting. Under the robe I discover a small piece of fading yellow paper, with a note written in a scrawl that even an ace handwriting analyst couldn't pin on anyone specific.

Clever. I walk over to the pay phone on the wall and beep into my messages, waiting to hear a familiar voice saying, "Surprise, the gift's from me!" Instead my lone message is from an old black man with a throaty Louis Armstrong–like growl.

"Hey, yeah, I'm calling to give you your next destination."

He rattles off an address that's over a half hour drive towards downtown, then adds, "And Mama, bring that robe you holdin' and hurry now. You got a six o'clock appointment. Don't be late."

I sit down on the tile floor, and for the first time in months, I start to laugh. Then come the questions. Should I actually run off to some mysterious unknown location just because an unidentified man told me to? What if this is some elaborate plot to harm me? Or worse, some lame practical joke? Maybe it's a wild goose chase leading to nowhere, sent from someone I know in a misguided attempt to lure me out of my heartbroken funk?

Intrigued as I am, I'm not sure I'm up for this. Frankly at this point I'd prefer to put on my new robe, go to the bedding department, and cuddle up on a Serta floor model. But the sleuth in me wins out over the jilted ex-lover in me, and I decide to head downtown.

While driving south on the Hollywood freeway, I ponder "The Case of the Inexplicable Birthday Treasure Hunt." Too bad I can't just peek in the back of the book to solve this one.

It could be from Danielle. Even though she is involved with "mole bitch," we still constantly talk about trying to see if we can make it work again. Maybe this is her way of taking the plunge, proving to me things could be different, that we don't have to take each other for granted the way we had toward the end, that the future might hold exciting surprises. . . .

On the other hand, it could also be from Nora. Sexy, fun, spiritual, creative, adventurous, and compassionate, Nora possesses every quality I ever dreamed of in a lover. Well, except for two: she isn't Danielle, and I'm not in love with her.

It also could have been dreamed up by one of my many brilliant, supportive friends who all know it's been a tough breakup for me.

Maybe one of them is trying to cheer me up on my first birthday in five years without Danielle.

I head east on Beverly until I finally find the address on a nondescript cement building sandwiched between a hand car wash and a piñata outlet store. As I pull into the parking lot, I notice two children crossing the street. One is holding a set of bongos, the other an Ouija board. Everyone is suspect.

I carry my robe into the building, where scents of jasmine and lavender greet me. A sign behind the counter informs me that I am at a spa, one that features mineral hot springs. A perky Chinese woman in a white lab coat smiles. "Hello. Can I hep you?" she asks in a heavy accent.

"Uh, yeah, I think I might have a six o'clock appointment for something?"

"You name?"

"Hillary Carlip."

"Oh, sure, sure. Come on. You got robe? Good, good."

The woman leads me into a locker room. "You not have much time for soak. You scrub in fifteen minutes," she says as she hands me a key to a locker and leaves.

I look around, hoping to find someone familiar lounging with a towel turban on her head, waiting to surprise me. But all I see are completely naked strangers. At least my mystery gift giver knows me well enough to realize I'm not going to parade around nude in front of anyone. I inconspicuously slip off my clothes, swaddle the terrycloth robe around me like a heliophobe on a trip to the beach, then venture out to find whatever it is I'm supposed to soak in.

Once I round the corner, I gasp at the sight. A stone cave with tropical plants growing inside, surrounds a pond of steaming mineral water. A small bridge crosses over the water, with vines clutching and twisting on it. Next to this glorious grotto I see two steam rooms—one featuring a thick foggy mist, the other dry and hot, smelling of eucalyptus. Several naked women sit soaking in the hot pond. I stand and watch as one climbs out, immerses herself in a smaller cold pool, and sighs with pleasure. The place is an Eden of steaming lushness. Checking to make sure no one is looking, I slip off my robe and ease into the near-boiling water. Thoughts give way to pure sensation and I soak in the nowness for what later feels like a long while. I am only startled back to my mind when an elderly Chinese woman calls my name, breaking the silence.

I climb out and follow the crone who is wearing a sheet wrapped around her waist and nothing on top—her large, sagging breasts flopping proudly as if they own the joint. She leads me through an archway of stone, part of the cave, to a large slab of granite, thigh high, and points for me to lie down on it. No talking here. Just dripping, splashing, lapping, quenching water. The woman applies a slimy, smooth grit of what feels like kelp and sand combined to my body and vigorously scrubs my skin with some sort of scouring pad. At first, losing an entire layer of my epidermis is painful. But as I literally shed my skin, I begin to feel free, more relaxed than I've felt in ages. I want to raise my head and say, "Thank you" to the old woman. Or, "This is great, you're great"—anything to acknowledge her, but I know that would interrupt the very intentional silence.

After a thorough scrubbing from head to toe, front and back, the woman sprays me down with soothing warm water from a green garden hose wound up like a jealous snake until all that is left is a slippery smooth, glowing body. In a tranquil trance I can barely whisper, "Thank you," but of course, I manage.

The woman smiles and winks at me. "Happy Birthday."

What?! Does *everyone* know? This snaps me right back from my body into my mind. Who's behind this? How? Why? This doesn't seem like Danielle's style—too thought-out and planned. But it's not really like Nora, either—she's far more understated.

Nora—shit! She's coming to my house at 7:30, in thirty minutes. I'll never make it home in time. I need to find a pay phone, and, despite being clad only in my robe, I dash from the grotto to the lobby packed with fully dressed men and women. I step into the phone booth and pull the door closed behind me. As I'm dialing Nora's number, it occurs to me to check my messages first. What if there's another "destination" that I'm being sent to tonight?

When I hear that I have one message, my heart beats quickly. Is it the excitement of the unknown, or is it, rather, the fact that I moved from pure relaxation to high panic in under thirty seconds?

"Hey it's me," Nora says on my machine. "Where are you?"

Like she doesn't know—Ha!

"I'm stuck at work and won't be able to get to your house till 8:30. Hope that's okay. I'll just pick up some food and bring it over and we'll have a Birthday Eve celebration. If that's not good, call me. Bye."

Hmmm. She sounded awfully nonchalant for someone who just arranged a complex birthday gift. So maybe Danielle is the culprit after all? Time to investigate. I dial Danielle's number.

"Hey," I say, trying to be casual.

"Hi, Honey," Danielle sounds excited. "What're you up to?"

"Like you don't know."

"What am I supposed to know?"

"You really don't know?"

"Know what? I might know if I knew what you were talking about."

"Jesus, it sounds like we're doing some vaudeville shtick." I sit down on the plastic seat. "Well, I'm kind of being sent on a treasure hunt."

"No way."

She really does sound clueless. "You swear you don't know anything about this?"

"Swear."

Still, I think as I pick at the threads of my new robe, Danielle has lied to me before—on more than one occasion—and she's good at it. She's a casting director, so maybe it's a skill developed from being around actors all day. So I don't rule her out completely.

"It's probably from *your new girlfriend*," she says mockingly.

"She's not my girlfriend. We're just dating."

"Yeah, right. So am I gonna see you tomorrow? Do I still have the three o'clock shift?" I smile when I realize it bothers her not to be the only one spending my birthday with me.

"Yeah. I'm looking forward to it."

"Me too." She pauses. "Honey?"

"Yeah?"

"I wish it was from me."

And so do I.

I hang up and return to the grotto. I wander into the steam room. Unable to see anyone in the thick mist, I hear deep exhales. I remember being twelve and going to the movies with my friend Diane Hutchings to see *Me, Natalie,* starring Patty Duke. Diane's mother dropped us at the theater a few minutes late; onscreen it was nighttime, and the theater was pitch black. In the dark I found a seat but accidentally sat down in a woman's lap. Throughout the rest of the movie Diane and I could not contain our laughter until, finally, the manager kicked us out. I don't want to repeat my mistake, especially now that I am in a place with all *naked bodies*. So I stand still, breathing in the generous gift someone—*whoever it is*—has bestowed upon me.

When I go to the locker room to dress, I discover a note has been left in my locker. Written in the same scrawl, on the same yellow paper, with the same purple pen as the last one, this one says:

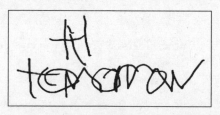

I race up my street just in time to meet Nora who has brought with her a Middle Eastern take-out feast: chicken kabobs slathered with a thick, garlicky paste; baba ghanoush; falafel balls; and neon pink pickled turnips, which I take off my plate and put on hers.

I tell her about the hunt, asking if she's behind it, but she becomes distant. She's convinced it's from Danielle. I tell her that the last note I received makes me think it's going to continue tomorrow, and she gets annoyed. She's made a 10:00 a.m. brunch reservation, and since she only has until 3:00 p.m. to be with me, then I go off with Danielle, she wants to make sure she has her time. I assure her that even if the hunt continues, I'll keep our plans.

The next morning the phone rings at 8:00 a.m. and this time it's "Mrs. Street," a woman with an English accent. She instructs me to go to my "next destination," the Sunrise Villa on Fairfax and Melrose, and to be there no later than 9:00 a.m. When Mrs. Street won't tell me who's behind this, I ask her to thank whoever it is but to inform them that I won't be able to go. After I hang up I grill Nora and, once again, she swears she knows nothing. Then, unexpectedly, she tells me I should continue with the hunt.

"Why? We have plans."

"You think I'm gonna stop you?" she says. "No way. You'd only resent it *and* me. We'll go to brunch after."

I thank her profusely for understanding, all the while wondering if I'm being had. I find Sunrise Villa in the phone book, call back Mrs. Street, then head out to destination unknown.

Sunrise Villa turns out to be a retirement home. All my friends and lovers are aware of the soft spot I have for old people. Those moments of vulnerability where authenticity peeks through touch me at my core. Or perhaps being sent here is to put my birthday in perspective? To show me that as old as approaching thirty feels now, it's so young in the scheme of things.

"You must be Hillary," a woman says in the same British accent I heard earlier on the phone.

"Mrs. Street?"

"Yes, come with me." We walk down a hallway that smells of disinfectant and burnt veal.

"Could you just tell me who sent me here?" I ask. "*Please.*"

"Sorry."

Before I can probe further, she throws open a door to a large, barren room full of old men and women, most in wheelchairs. They look right at me and burst into song. "Happy birthday to you, happy birthday to you. . . . "

A nurse wheels an industrial silver cart toward me. I start crying as I look down at a cake, candles aflame, with icing that reads: "Happy Birthday Hillary."

"Happy birthday, dear. . . . " The elderly folks stumble over the name, no one quite sure who they are celebrating. "Happy birthday to you."

Then comes the chanting: "CAKE. CAKE. CAKE," they demand as they tap their hands on tables and wheelchair arms.

A tiny woman in a big yellow sunhat calls out, "Make a wish, make a wish."

I close my eyes. What do I even wish for? That I find out who sent me here? That Danielle and I get back together and make it work? Or that my heart forgets about her and gives itself over to Nora?

I know. *Clarity.* I will wish for clarity.

I blow out the candles.

I spend an hour with Lil and Harriet, Marvin and Troy, and the rest of the seniors who are thrilled to have company. I hear tales of lives lived, love discovered, and hearts broken. When I leave, I thank everyone for making my birthday so special and vow to visit again.

Mrs. Street meets me in the foyer. "You're to call home now," she says. "And happy birthday."

I beep into my answering machine and listen to seven birthday messages—the first from Danielle, then my mom and dad, Howard, my old friend Greg, and two other friends. The last message is a familiar voice—it's *Mrs. Street*, who happens to be standing just three feet away from me. Amusing.

In her proper British accent she says, "A bear has shit in the woods.

Can you find him? Try Griffith Park." By the time I hang up, Mrs. Street has vanished.

I call Nora and tell her of my dilemma, of the puzzling, indecipherable next clue.

"Go ahead and just finish whatever this is," she says, trying to conceal her upset. "But if it goes past my time, I think you should reschedule Danielle for later. Don't you?"

"Absolutely," I say. "Thanks for being so cool."

Relieved, I head to Griffith Park. I remember seeing a statue of a bear at the Los Feliz entrance. When I arrive and find the statue, I see an envelope placed under the bear's ass. Inside the envelope is a small key and a note:

My heart begins to pound, my mind races. This is it, I am sure, the moment I will discover who the genius behind "The Case of the Inexplicable Birthday Treasure Hunt" actually is. Will Danielle be standing there, begging me to come back to her? Or Nora, helping me to forget all about Danielle? Or maybe it's someone I haven't even considered? It could be anyone, I realize, and it's about time I found out.

I continue up the path and approach an oak tree. I scream when

I suddenly see someone I know very well—in fact, it's someone I have been living with for seven years. It's Sally—*a child mannequin from my collection of department store mannequins.* She's chained to a tree. I fall to the ground, laughing my ass off.

When I calm down I discover a note pinned to my old sixties Snoopy sweatshirt that Sally wears over her tasteful vintage corduroy jumper.

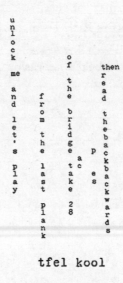

```
unlock me and let's play   of the bridge take 28   then read the back backwards
                 from the last plank        paces
```

```
tfel kool
```

I unlock the lock with the key from the last envelope, then unwrap twenty feet of chain from Sally and the tree. I drape the chain over my shoulder and continue on, carrying Sally. What a sight I must be, a stunned grown woman draped in heavy chains, carrying a child mannequin, counting paces, and staring at backwards writing, talking out loud: "TFEL KOOL. Look left!"

And I do. There, on a fence, is a large sign written in black marker.

things a little rocky?
look right

I turn my head to the right, and see a pile of rocks, with another note on the top of the heap.

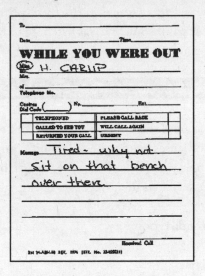

I creep along, checking the bushes, waiting for someone to appear. Sally and I sit on the bench. When I look up, I see another huge sign tacked to another aged oak tree.

Don't just sit there. Look under your ass

I lean over, and, just as I'm about to nab the manila envelope beneath the bench, my hand touches someone else's hand. I sit up fast.

Standing next to me is a middle-aged man in a baseball cap, his eyes droopy. "Hey!" he says at the same time I do.

"That's for me," I declare, wondering if he's just a plant, all part of this cooked-up scheme.

"How do you know it's yours?" he asks defensively.

I point to the clue in my hand, the chains draped over my shoulder and the mannequin I'm sitting next to. "DUH!" I can't help but say.

He looks disappointed but hands me the manila envelope and walks away.

There's a Dynamo label stuck on the front of the envelope that makes me shiver. It's as if someone was listening to my birthday wish at Sunrise Villa.

TO BE USED FOR CLARITY

I tear open the envelope. Inside I find a pair of eyeglasses, which feature, in place of lenses, winky eyes that shift from one picture to another with each tiny movement. The first image looks like eyes until I move the glasses; then the image is a pin-up girl. Entertaining, but now what?

I sit, waiting for direction.

Nothing.

I try on the glasses.

That's where I find the next clue—taped to the inside of each lens.

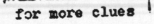 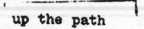

for more clues · up the path

I heave Sally up off the bench and we head uphill. Atop a drinking fountain I spot yet one more sign.

Who's your friend?
Check her pocket.

I reach into my child mannequin's corduroy jumper pocket and pull out a piece of paper.

**Bet you and Sally
are starved
Look up the road
and find your reward**

I spot it up ahead. A blanket. And there, spread out across the blanket, is a basket of biscuits and muffins, strawberry jam, orange and pink ceramic bowls filled with nectarines and figs, and in the center an enormous bouquet of lilies, tulips, and freesias. It's all surrounded by several gifts brilliantly wrapped in Gift Wrap Option C.

I feel nauseous with anticipation. I look around. No one's in sight.

Then I spot one more note tucked in the basket of muffins.

**HAPPY BIRTHDAY - SORRY I
COULDN'T BE THERE WITH YOU.**

No way! Shit. Okay, I can't take this anymore. I can't wait any longer. Who's behind this? How long will it keep going? How will it end?

I take a breath and stop myself. Why do any of those things matter when the hunt itself is so phenomenal? I breathe again, and this time, with my exhale, *I release the need to know*. I take a biscuit from the basket, slather it with jam, and begin to enjoy my birthday breakfast.

Then I hear a voice—faintly at first. It's a woman's voice. She's singing "Happy Birthday." I stand, cock my head, and hear that the song is coming from the bushes. As it gets louder and closer, I hold my breath. Who will it be?

And there, into the clearing, steps *Nora*.

"No fucking way!" I screech. "Damn, you're a good liar!"

She laughs. I take her in my arms. "Thank you, thank you, thank you," I keep repeating. "That was absolutely amazing. You're amazing."

We share breakfast and talk about the hunt and her stellar acting job. I even open the presents—in front of her—having learned a good lesson in receiving the past two days.

We spend a lovely day together, and later I spend a long, teary but sweet night with Danielle. But when Danielle asks if she can sleep over, I shake my head.

"I need to be alone," I say. And I realize I actually mean it.

At midnight I crawl under the covers, close my eyes, and think over every detail of "The Case of the Inexplicable Birthday Treasure Hunt."

I can't help but smile. My birthday wish has come true. *I have clarity.* As spectacular as my gift was, and as much as I want Nora to be "the one," I'm not in love with her. We can't *make* someone into our soul mate. If we could, it would have nothing to do with our souls. And maybe the person we think is "the one," like Danielle, is just one of the destinations and gifts along the way that ultimately lead us to solving the mystery.

I turn on my side and glance at my cowboy lamp. And then, for the first time in twenty-nine years, I reach over and turn off the light.

1989

* Ayatollah Khomeini offers 2.5 million dollars for the murder of *The Satanic Verses* author, Salman Rushdie. The press claims that Yusuf Islam, who I saw perform countless times at the Troub when he was Cat Stevens, endorses the fatwa on Rushdie's life. "Oh, baby, baby it's a Wild World. . . . "

* Keanu Reeves, a close friend of Katie's, my girlfriend of two years, who filled her cupboards with groceries and endless boxes of macaroni and cheese when she was broke, scores a hit with *Bill and Ted's Excellent Adventure.*

* *Beverly Hills Cop*s are busy after Lyle and Eric Menendez shoot their wealthy parents to death in their family's den and Zsa Zsa Gabor is arrested after slapping a motorcycle police officer.

* After two years of intense ACT UP protests over the high price for the drug AZT, proven to delay the onset of AIDS, the drug company Burroughs Wellcome lowers the price by 20 percent. Many of my friends and acquaintances die of AIDS, as does Amanda Blake, Miss Kitty on *Gunsmoke.*

* I mourn the loss of Lucille Ball, who dies at age seventy-seven.

✽ Still a *Knots Landing* fan, I befriend one of the show's regulars, Teri Austin, whose character turns into a psychopath and dresses in a wig and disguise to kill Valene Ewing. Teri shows up at my birthday party in the psycho murderess disguise.

✽ A group of friends gather at my house to watch the infamous Rob Lowe sex videotape.

✽ After experiencing too many headaches and bursts of energy followed by crashes of exhaustion, I give up my dessert habit and stop eating sugar, and all sweeteners, entirely.

✽ Teenage pop sensation Debbie Gibson, the youngest artist in chart history to have written, produced, and performed a #1 song, co-hosts the *American Music Awards*.

Tyro Scribes Sell Spec for Big Bucks

INT. GREAT WESTERN FORUM, LOS ANGELES, 1989 — NIGHT

CLOSE ON HILLARY CARLIP, early thirties, an artistic brunette woman who exudes warmth and creativity, sitting in the audience at a concert. Next to her is PAUL AARON, a movie producer with a kind, open face.

PULL BACK TO REVEAL THE SINGER ONSTAGE. It's teen pop sensation DEBBIE GIBSON, singing her hit song, "ONLY IN MY DREAMS."

> HILLARY
> (under her breath, to Paul)
> Only in my dreams. . . . Ain't that the fuckin' truth.

LYNDA OBST, another producer, sits with Hillary and Paul. She stands up along with teens in the audience, dancing and clapping. An intense woman in her forties, Lynda seems like she's always buzzed on coke, even when she's not.

LYNDA
(shouting over to Paul)
Look at how everybody loves Debbie Gibson! And
she's all ours!

FLASHBACK: One year earlier. Hillary is sitting
in the living room of her 1910 Craftsman house
with KATIE, her live-in girlfriend of two years. A
brilliant writer, Katie leaves herself wide open to
access that deep creativity which not only lets her
humor and insight shine, it also often lets out her
fear and darkness. The two are collaborating on a
screenplay.

HILLARY
I don't think Betty would have a problem
approaching the Flames once she sees them
dancing. She doesn't know yet that they're a
gang.

KATIE
Yeah, but it's 1964, she's just moved to the
Bronx, and the Flames are black girls. Do you
think she ever knew any black girls in the
suburbs of Scarsdale?

HILLARY
Her maid's daughter?

KATIE
Exactly.

The two, entwined on the couch like a scene out
of the movie *Love Story*, minus the fatal illness,
continue writing.

MONTAGE: BELINDA CARLISLE'S "HEAVEN IS A PLACE ON EARTH" PLAYS as we see:

—Hillary and Katie hug each other and jump and shout as they finish their screenplay. Their big, brown hound dog, MONSTER, joins in, jumping and barking in celebration.

—CLOSE ON SCRIPT COVER, we see the title of the film, *SKIRTS*. We also see that it's the "SEVENTH DRAFT." Hillary rips the cover off and replaces it with one that says "FIRST DRAFT."

—Hillary and Katie meet with producer Paul Aaron at his office. He's going over the script with them and is clearly enthusiastic about it.

—At the door of Paul's office, Hillary greets old friend KENNY ORTEGA, choreographer of *Xanadu* and *Dirty Dancing*, and now a director. She introduces him to Paul and Katie. They all talk excitedly and laugh--clearly a partnership is forming.

—Hillary, Katie, Paul, and Kenny walk into CAA, Creative Artists Agency, in Beverly Hills. They shake hands with several agents, who are all gushing over the script.

—We see various QUICK CUTS of STUDIO EXECUTIVES reading the script, then immediately picking up the phone to call CAA with offers.

—QUICK CUTS of Hillary and Katie at home receiving gifts: A muffin basket. Flowers. Caps, shot glasses, sweatshirts, T-shirts, mugs, and key chains--all with different studio logos on them.

—See the cover of *Daily Variety* spin into frame, its headlines shouting "BIDDING WAR FOR *SKIRTS*. TYRO SCRIBES SELL SPEC FOR BIG BUCKS."

—MONTAGE ENDS as Hillary and Katie hug triumphantly.

INT. COLUMBIA STUDIOS - DAWN STEEL'S OFFICE - DAY

Hillary and Katie sit close to each other, along with Paul and Kenny, as they meet with the infamous DAWN STEEL, the first female ever to head a movie studio. She's imposing but effusive, wearing, in her power suit jacket pocket, an auburn-colored scarf that matches the color of her hair exactly.

AMY PASCAL, the sharp yet warm VICE PRESIDENT, and other male EXECUTIVES sit around the conference table, all part of the meeting.

> DAWN
> We know you had several other offers, and we're thrilled you chose to work with us.

> AMY
> We're all so excited about *Skirts,* and we'll do everything we can to see that the film gets made.

> EXECUTIVE #1
> Absolutely.

> EXECUTIVE #2
> It's a priority.

                    DAWN
I want to introduce you girls to the Executive
Producer we're attaching to the project. We
think she's perfect for *Skirts* and I'm sure
you'll agree. Lynda Obst.

Lynda enters, clicking in on high heels. Though she
comes off sweet and accessible, there's a look in
her eye that explains why people have said she's
got "killer instincts." She shakes hands with
everyone then gives Dawn and Amy each an air kiss.

                    LYNDA
            (to Hillary and Katie)
So great to meet you girls. I fell in love
with your script. I could totally relate to
Betty and the fish-out-of-water aspect.

                    AMY
I personally loved how the girl gangs used
dancing to establish their hierarchy.

                  EXECUTIVE #1
What I thought was so brilliant was setting
it all against the backdrop of the New York
World's Fair--especially with their motto that
year: "Peace Through Understanding."

                    DAWN
Basically we're saying we absolutely loved
every word of your script.

                   HILLARY
Cool.

                         KATIE
     Great.

                         PAUL
     So that must mean there won't be anything
     really for the girls to rewrite.

                         LYNDA
     Well, we do have a few notes.

ANGLE ON Lynda passing out copies of notes to
everyone in the room.

CLOSE ON THE PAPERS in Hillary's hands as she leafs
through *twenty pages of single-spaced typed notes.*

                         LYNDA (CONT'D)
     And since the film's on a fast track, we'd
     like you to get the rewrite in to us within a
     month.

                         AMY
     We know you girls can do it.

                                             CUT TO:

INT. HILLARY AND KATIE'S HOUSE - DAY

The girls are working at a desk in an upstairs
office. Out the window we can see the Hollywood
sign looming in the background. We come in on the
tail end of an argument.

                         HILLARY
     Okay . . . this isn't even about the script,
     is it? What's with you? This should be the
     happiest time of our lives!

                    KATIE

I don't know . . . it's just . . .

                    HILLARY

You're so depressed lately. What's going on?

                    KATIE

I guess I feel pressured--with work on the
show . . .
(pan to a framed photo of the *Family Ties* logo
featuring Katie's "written by" credit)
     . . . and our deadline. I'm only twenty-three,
and I have all these huge responsibilities.

                    HILLARY

Can I do anything to help?

                    KATIE

No, no.

Hillary takes a sip of coffee, giving silence in
hopes that Katie will take advantage of it and say
more. She finally does.

                KATIE (CONT'D)

It's not just that. . . . I love you so much,
but I feel like I've lost my independence.

Hillary almost does a spit take with her beverage.
She's definitely felt some distance from Katie over
the past few months, but she just thought they were
going through a temporary rough patch.

                    HILLARY

So what are you saying?

                    KATIE
I need some time alone. Need to go find
myself.

                    HILLARY
Wouldn't it be easier if you had someone
helping you look?

                    KATIE
I'm serious. I think I should get my own
place.

PUSH IN CLOSE ON HILLARY, disbelief on her face.

FADE TO BLACK.

FADE UP ON Hillary helping Katie find an apartment.

QUICK CUTS of several completely wrong places--
roaches in the bathtub, noisy neighbors downstairs,
a view of the neighbors' bedroom directly outside
the window.

END ON Katie finding a beautiful place and signing
a lease. Hillary excuses herself, goes into Katie's
new bathroom, sits on the edge of the bathtub, and
weeps.

INT. COLUMBIA STUDIOS OFFICE - A MONTH LATER - DAY

Paul sits between Hillary and Katie. We can tell
things are strained between the girls. Lynda, Amy,
and one of the Executives are going over notes.

                    AMY
You guys did a great job with the rewrite.

Hillary Carlip

> LYNDA

Dawn's maid read the script, you know, to give
a black perspective. . . .

The girls can't help but look at each other.

> EXECUTIVE #1

Her only problem was one of the Flames'
names--Cloretta. She felt that character's
name needs to be changed.

> HILLARY

That's it? She didn't like the name Cloretta?

> PAUL

Look, if that's the only note she had, then
we're thrilled.

> LYNDA

Yes, that's it from her. But the studio has a
few more notes for you.

She passes them around to all.

CLOSE ON THE PAPERS in Hillary's hands as she leafs
through *ten pages of single-spaced typed notes*.

Paul, the girls' champion and protector, speaks
out.

> PAUL

The script keeps getting further and further
away from what it was you all loved about it
to begin with.

> KATIE
> (chiming in)

It feels like it's losing its essence.

HILLARY

It's no longer our vision.

LYNDA

You know how few movies in development get made. Do you want to get *Skirts* green-lit or what?

AMY

Why don't you girls dive in and we'll reconvene a week from tomorrow.

CUT TO:

EXT. COLUMBIA STUDIOS PARKING LOT - MOMENTS LATER

Hillary and Katie are leaning against a car.

HILLARY

This is so bizarre. Going home to separate places.

KATIE

But we have a date tomorrow night.

HILLARY

Somehow that's not very comforting. I don't know if I can do this--go from living together for two years to dating.

KATIE

Can we at least try?

HILLARY

Fine. So I guess I'll just see you tomorrow night.

                              KATIE

    I'll call you in the morning, and we'll figure
    out a work schedule for this week.

    There's an awkward moment before they move to hug
    each other. They kiss good-bye and head their
    separate ways.

                                              CUT TO:

    INT. HILLARY'S BEDROOM - NIGHT

    Hillary lies on the bed with Monster watching the
    American Music Awards on TV.

    As the Favorite Pop/Rock album is announced--the
    soundtrack to *Dirty Dancing*--she picks up the phone
    and dials. We HEAR A RING and KATIE ANSWERS.

                              KATIE
                         (on the phone)
       Hello?

                             HILLARY
       Hey. You watching the *American Music Awards*?
       Kenny's movie just won Best Album.

                              KATIE
    Uh . . . yeah. I saw.

    Hillary senses something's up.

                             HILLARY
       Are you okay? Why do you sound so weird?

                              KATIE
       Do I?
                    (a little too enthusiastic)
       I'm fine!

                    HILLARY
What's going on?

                    KATIE
Nothing. I'm just in the middle of something.
Can I call you later?

A look washes over Hillary's face. She sits up.

                    HILLARY
Someone's totally there with you. Who's there?

                    KATIE
No one. I'll call you a bit later. Okay?

                    HILLARY
Oh my God. You're totally seeing someone,
aren't you?

Silence on the other end of the phone.

                    HILLARY (CONT'D)
          (stands up--she can't hold back)
How dare you! You need to be independent and
you're seeing someone else like five seconds
after you move out?! You need space MY ASS! I
can't fucking believe you!

She slams down the phone. Sits back down on the bed
in shock. The phone rings. She picks the receiver
up and hangs it up immediately. This happens two
more times. Finally . . .

                    HILLARY (CONT'D)
WHAT?!?!?

INT. KATIE'S APARTMENT LIVING ROOM - SAME TIME

Katie is crying. ANOTHER WOMAN tiptoes away into
the other room.

> KATIE
> I'm so sorry. I swear this just happened in
> the last few days. I never cheated on you.
> > (barely stopping for a breath)
> I still love you. I just can't be tied down
> right now. Please forgive me.

CUT TO:

MONTAGE:

—We see Hillary on a plane. She sits with
headphones on, trying to block out any thoughts
with her music.

—Now in a taxi, Hillary is driving through snow. Hard
to tell which is darker--the storming winter sky or
Hillary's mood as they pull up to a loft in Soho.

—Hillary is greeted by her artist friend LENI who
hugs her and welcomes her into her bright, colorful
loft.

EXT. WORLD'S FAIR SITE - QUEENS - DAY

Hillary and Leni, both bundled up in scarves,
hats, and mittens, tread through the snow at the
old World's Fair site, taking in the few remaining
structures and relics of the 1964 World's Fair.

> LENI
> I'm really glad you came to visit, though I'm
> so sorry about the circumstances.

                         HILLARY
        Thanks. It's good to get out of L.A.

They walk into what was the New York State
Pavilion. Covering the ground is a huge map of New
York inlaid in gorgeous terrazzo—colored marble.
They look at it in awe.

                          LENI
        So how are you and Katie gonna keep working
        together? You're still not finished with
        rewrites, are you?

                         HILLARY
        No. In fact, the minute I get back I have to
        see her--at a *meeting* at *Columbia*. I don't
        know how I'm gonna hold it together.

Leni puts her arm around Hillary as they continue
walking. They arrive at the Unisphere, the famous
enormous steel globe which once greeted all
visitors to the Fair.

                     HILLARY (CONT'D)
        Wow.

                          LENI
        It's so amazing that it's still here.

Hillary looks at the plaque below the Unisphere
and reads the motto of the fair written on it, the
theme of the film she and Katie have been working
on for two years now.

CLOSE ON PLAQUE: "Peace Through Understanding."

Hillary rolls her eyes.

Hillary Carlip

INT. COLUMBIA STUDIOS - DAY

Katie is already at the table when Hillary walks in. Hillary says a general hello to all, then sits as far away from Katie as possible, never once looking at her.

Paul, Lynda, Amy, and the Executives are all in attendance.

                    LYNDA
    WE LOVE THIS SCRIPT!!

                    HILLARY
    Let me guess . . . you have a few notes.

                                    SMASH CUT:

CLOSE ON PAPERS in Hillary's hands as she leafs through *eight pages of single-spaced typed notes.*

MONTAGE:

Hillary and Katie do rewrites--with Paul always there, acting as a buffer. The girls barely speak. Hillary looks like she's still pissed off and just trying to keep it all together. Katie alternates between looking totally sad and numb.

INT. HILLARY'S HOUSE - OFFICE - A MONTH LATER - DAY

Hillary is sitting at her desk writing when the phone rings.

                    HILLARY
    Hello?

WE HEAR PAUL'S VOICE on the phone.

PAUL
(excitedly)
CONGRATULATIONS!! *Skirts* got the green light
today. They're making your movie!

HILLARY
Really? Swear?

PAUL
Yep. I'm so proud of you guys. You and Katie
should be so happy.

ON Hillary's face, a combo platter of emotions.

FADE OUT as the cover of *Daily Variety* FADES IN:
"IT'S A GO FOR COLUMB PREXY'S PET PROJECT *SKIRTS*."

CUT TO:

INT. PAUL'S OFFICE - A MONTH LATER

Hillary sits with Paul and Kenny, getting updated.

KENNY
I'm sorry Katie couldn't be here, but it's
great she sold a TV show in Toronto.

PAUL
Yeah, she'll be there for the next several
months. It'll be good for her to go back home
for a bit.

Hillary couldn't look more relieved.

PAUL (CONT'D)
So, Kenny and I have a lot to catch you up on.

                    HILLARY
Lay it on me.

                    PAUL
Well, there's good news and bad news.

Hillary takes a breath. She's ready to hear.

                    KENNY
Debbie Gibson's been cast as the lead.

                    HILLARY
What?! Is that the good news or the bad news?

                    PAUL
I know, she's not really how we pictured the
character.

                    HILLARY
She's really talented but I believe the
description of Betty is "sexy and hot." Not
really words I'd use for "pop-princess" Debbie
Gibson. And can she dance?

                    KENNY
You leave that to me. I'll have her dancing.

                    PAUL
Look, the studio didn't want to go with an
unknown, and Debbie's the most famous teen
girl today. I think it's a smart move.

                    HILLARY
Okay, if that's the good news, should I take a
pill before the bad news?

KENNY

Wait. One other thing. We're starting to
audition dancers tomorrow. I want you to be
there.

HILLARY

Wow. I'd love to! How exciting.
                    (beat)
So, come on, you're killin' me here. Bad news?

PAUL
                (takes a deep breath)
Lynda hired Richard LaGravenese to do a polish
of the script.

HILLARY
                (in disbelief)
What?

PAUL

I'm sorry, Hill. The studio wants you guys off
the project.

HILLARY

You're kidding, right? We did every single
note they asked for. What more can be
polished?

PAUL

It's Lynda. She's been working with Richard,
he's been having a lot of success, and she
wants him to take a pass at the script.

He stands up and goes over to Hillary.

PAUL (CONT'D)

Don't worry. I'll show you what he's doing and
if you and Katie want to do any fixes, I'll
take them in and say they're from me.

HILLARY

I can't believe this. One minute they're
kissing our asses and then the next they
fire us from our own movie and hire someone
to rewrite it without even telling us! THAT
SUCKS!

PAUL

Welcome to showbiz.

CUT TO:

INT. DANCE STUDIO - DAY

Paul sits in between Hillary and Lynda. Kenny
demonstrates a dance routine while a room full of
girls--black, white, Hispanic, Italian--all learn
the moves. The girls are brilliantly dressed like
they're all in gangs in 1964.

QUICK CUTS:

—Kenny splitting the girls into groups of ten.

—Kenny working with each group as they learn the
moves.

—Hillary talks to Paul, but she and Lynda barely
say a word to each other.

—Kenny calls the groups up one at a time, and they
all do the routine flawlessly.

It's absolutely amazing. The intensity of seeing
a gang of girls kicking ass with powerful dance
moves, bringing the essence of *Skirts* to life, is
overwhelming, especially for Hillary.

> HILLARY
> (to Paul, holding back tears)
> I wish Katie were here to see this.

CUT TO:

EXT. PAUL'S BACKYARD - A FEW WEEKS LATER -
AFTERNOON

Hillary helps Paul set out plates of hors
d'oeuvres.

> PAUL
> I wanted to get you up to speed before
> everyone arrives. We've been doing some
> casting and have found some terrific people.

> HILLARY
> That's great! Like who?

> PAUL
> For Juanita we cast Rosie Perez, who was just
> in Spike Lee's film *Do the Right Thing*. . . .

> HILLARY
> She's fantastic!

> PAUL
> And for Monica and Fabio, a couple of
> unknowns--Marisa Tomei and David Schwimmer.
> I'm sorry you can't come see the screen tests.

                    HILLARY
  Why can't I?

Paul stalls a bit, wiping some crumbs off the
table.

                      PAUL
  Lynda has Richard sitting in.

                    HILLARY
  No fucking way! None of this would be
  happening without my idea and our script. I
  thought he was just hired to "polish" it,
  and you're telling me that HE'S part of the
  casting and we're not? This is so fucked up!

We hear a VOICE call from the backyard gate.

                  LYNDA (O.S.)
  Helloooo!

Hillary ties to contain herself. Paul opens the
gate and there's Lynda standing with a MAN. Paul
and the man give a warm hug--they know each other.
Lynda sees Hillary.

                LYNDA (CONT'D)
  Oh, I didn't know you were coming with us
  tonight.

Hillary can barely get out a greeting as Lynda and
the man walk in.

                LYNDA (CONT'D)
  Hillary, this is Richard LaGravenese.

                    HILLARY
              (pulling herself together)
    Hey, nice to meet you.

                    RICHARD
    You too. You guys wrote a great script.

Thinking, "then why are you here?" Hillary just
says, politely:

                    HILLARY
    Thanks.

                                        CUT TO:

INT. GREAT WESTERN FORUM - BACK TO PRESENT DAY

Hillary sits next to Paul, who sits next to Lynda,
who sits next to Richard, all in the audience
watching Debbie Gibson. The crowd goes wild as
Debbie finishes her concert.

                    DEBBIE
              (from the stage)
    Thank you so much. Good night, everyone!

Thunderous applause and standing ovations.

                                    DISSOLVE TO:

INT. FORUM CLUB - LATER

An after-concert party is in progress. There's a
long line of people waiting to talk to Debbie.
Lynda grabs Richard by the hand, takes him over,
and cuts to the front of the line. Hillary and Paul
tag along.

Lynda hugs Debbie.

Hillary Carlip

What a fantastic show! Just wait 'till all
your fans see you shine in *Skirts*!

DEBBIE

Thanks! I'm so excited!

LYNDA

Debbie, I want you to meet the writer of
Skirts.

Hillary smiles, starts to move toward Debbie. But
she's cut off by Lynda who continues:

LYNDA (CONT'D)

This is Richard LaGravenese.

DEBBIE

Hey Richard. So happy to meet you. I can't
tell you how much I love this script.

SLOW PAN OVER to Hillary who looks like she's been
kicked in the gut. Oh wait, she *has* been.

CUT TO:

EXT. MELISSA ETHERIDGE'S BACKYARD – AFTERNOON –
MONTHS LATER

Hillary is at a party filled with attractive gay
women. ELIZABETH, a striking brunette, brooding and
dark, is flirting with Hillary. MELISSA ETHERIDGE,
with short spiky hair, brings the woman over and
introduces her to Hillary.

MONTAGE of Hillary going out with her new
girlfriend, ELIZABETH.

—At a concert together.

—At a cabin by a lake.

—Driving in a convertible down the streets of L.A.

—Calendar pages flip, six months passing.

CUT TO:

HEADLINES SPIN INTO FRAME:

—*Daily Variety*: "SONY BUYS COLUMBIA. GUBER-PETERS SET AS CO-CHAIRMEN."

We see more of the article: "Whether Dawn Steel will remain at Col is unclear. In any case, one of her films, *Skirts*, starring Debbie Gibson, is safe. Picture is fully crewed and cast, set to start filming in Los Angeles shortly."

—*New York Daily News* spins into frame. We see: "*SKIRTS* . . . VICTIM OF STUDIO POLITICS: DEBBIE GIBSON'S CHAMPION, COLUMBIA PICTURES PREZ DAWN STEEL, IS RUMORED TO BE ON HER WAY OUT."

—*The Hollywood Reporter* spins in, its headline says: "GUBER, PETERS DROP STEEL'S *SKIRTS* PIC."

CUT TO:

INT. HILLARY'S HOUSE - BEDROOM - DAY

Hillary lies on the bed; all the papers with headlines we've just seen surround her. It's clear she's been crying. She looks at the phone, hesitant. Finally she picks it up and dials.

WE HEAR THE PHONE RING and KATIE ANSWER.

                    KATIE
                 (on the phone)
    Hello?

                    HILLARY
    Hey. It's me. Did you talk to Paul?

                    KATIE
    Yeah. I can't believe it. I really wanted to
    call you but I thought. . . .

                    HILLARY
    I know.

                    KATIE
    Honey?
                 (beat)
    I'm so sorry. About everything.

                    HILLARY
    I know. Me too.

                                        CUT TO:

INT AIRPORT - ONE WEEK LATER - DAY

Katie gets off a plane and walks through the gate
into LAX.

CLOSE ON her face, filled with shock and delight as
she spots someone.

ANGLE ON Hillary, in a crowd of drivers who
all hold signs to pick up a specific passenger
arriving.

Hillary holds a sign, too. It says CLORETTA.

Katie dissolves into laughter and runs up to hug Hillary. They don't let go for a long time.

                                        CUT TO:

INT. THEATER - MONTHS LATER - NIGHT

ANGLE ON an audience. We see Katie sitting with Paul and Kenny in a small auditorium. Hillary's girlfriend Elizabeth sits with them, too.

The lights dim and Hillary walks out onto the stage. The audience applauds.

                    HILLARY
      Hey everyone. Thanks so much for coming
      tonight. When I started volunteering at
      Aviva, the residential treatment center
      for at-risk teenage girls, I was teaching
      creative writing. But as I spent more time
      with the girls, I realized there was a piece
      of material that would be perfect for them to
      appear in. So I'm proud to present the girls
      of Aviva starring in... *SKIRTS*!

MUSIC KICKS IN. The curtain goes up. Twelve teenage girls who've all really been in gangs, enter onstage. They start dancing, doing the routine that Kenny had choreographed at the *Skirts* dance auditions. The girls are as kick-ass and powerful as the professional dancers. What's more, they're the real deal, totally capturing the initial essence and vision of *Skirts*.

ANGLE ON Katie, Kenny, and Paul, who all couldn't be more thrilled.

Katie sees Hillary standing in the wings. Hillary catches Katie's eye, too. We see in their look that despite all they've been through--personally and professionally--everything's OK now, and they'll remain close friends and collaborators for a long time to come.

FADE OUT ON: The MUSIC THUMPING, the girls dancing, and the audience clapping along.

THE END

This is a fictitious screenplay based on actual events.

DAILY VARIETY

Los Angeles, CA 90036, Monday, Dec. 11, 1989

'Skirts' Tossed Into Turnaround

"Skirts," a Lynda Obst production greenlighted by Columbia Pictures president Dawn Steel — a pet project she helped put together — has been placed on turnaround by the studio's new Guber-Peters administration.

Picture was fully crewed and cast, set to start filming in Los Angeles in six weeks. Film, toplining rock star Debbie Gibson and Rose Perez of "Do The Right Thing," was to be directed by Kenny Orte-

(Continued on Page 19, Column 3)

THE REPORTER

Monday, December 11, 1989

Guber, Peters drop Steel's 'Skirts' pic

Seven weeks before principal photography was set to begin on Kenny Ortega's $12 million 1960s dance musical "Skirts," the pet project of studio president Dawn Steel has been put into turnaround by new Columbia heads Peter Guber and Jon Peters.

The film was to mark the directorial debut of choreographer Ortega ("Dirty Dancing") and pop princess Debbie Gibson's entrance into features.

— continued on page 24

NEW YORK'S HOMETOWN CONNECTION
DAILY NEWS

IT'S A VERY SOUR NOTE FOR DEBBIE

Poor Debbie Gibson. Long Island's top teen songstress was to star in "Skirts," a $12 million "Grease"-type flick set at the 1964 World's Fair. Shooting was planned for next month, but the project's a victim of studio politics: Debbie's champion, Columbia Pictures prez Dawn Steel, is rumored to be on her way out.

1990

* Ken, Sam, and I continue to rent our house out as a location for films, TV shows, and commercials. Bea Arthur sleeps in my bed, Billy Crystal tends our garden, and the entire exterior of our house is painted pink.

* At Farm Aid IV, Elton John dedicates "Candle in the Wind" to teenage AIDS patient Ryan White. White dies the next day. Ten more people I know succumb to the disease.

* Other endings: Nelson Mandela is set free from prison, signalling the end of apartheid in South Africa; President Bush and Soviet Union Leader Mikhail Gorbachev sign a treaty to end chemical weapon production; and Sammy Davis Jr. dies.

* The Fender Stratocaster that Jimi Hendrix used to perform his famous version of the "Star Spangled Banner" at Woodstock is auctioned for $295,000. My brother, still a huge Hendrix fan, and his wife give birth to their second child.

✱ A photographer friend is hired to take pictures of one of my favorite singers, Nina Simone, in Nina's L.A. apartment. I pose as a photographer's assistant so I can meet her.

✱ Unemployed and living on state benefits, J. K. Rowling comes up with the idea for *Harry Potter* while on a train ride from Manchester to London.

✱ Mötley Crüe's Tommy Lee is arrested for indecent exposure after mooning an audience during a concert in Georgia. Maybe now he'll stay out of trouble.

✱ After breaking up with Elizabeth, I take some time off from relationships. MC Hammer dominates the charts with "U Can't Touch This" and the top-grossing film of the year is *Home Alone*.

Madame Zola, Psychic to the Stars

I trip over a tricolored gnome lawn ornament that hovers protectively next to the front door, nowhere near any lawn. I obey the handwritten sign that reads "PLEASE NOCK" and I "nock."

A plump Eastern European woman dressed in stone-washed denim hot pants, a Lakers T-shirt, and rhinestone-studded high platform shoes greets me. She leads me into a small living room inside the stuffy house in the San Fernando Valley and gestures for me to take a seat beside her on the plastic-covered sofa. I have waited weeks for an available appointment and now *finally* I'm here with Madame Zola, Psychic to the Stars.

A familiar-looking brunette wearing a lot of gold jewelry sits across the room on a plastic-covered rocking chair. Will she be present during my reading? Who is she, anyway? I know I've seen her before somewhere.

Madame Zola offers me a butterscotch Lifesaver. I accept and suck away on it, anxiously waiting for our session to begin. But instead of divining my future, she turns toward a large console television set that blares from one corner of the room and settles in to watch the soap opera playing on it.

Then I get it. This is not Madame Zola, Psychic to the Stars. At least I *hope* it isn't.

I need guidance, and I need it now. I have never been at so many crossroads at once. I don't have a clue what to do next with my career—do I keep writing screenplays, which are lucrative but soul-crushing, in a business where it's nearly impossible to retain an original vision? Do I return to performing even though the audition process is humiliating and I've only managed to be cast in small roles in less-than-stellar projects? Do I keep writing but in some form other than movies? And my love life is in dire need of new direction as well. My last girlfriend, Elizabeth, turned out to be even more dark and draining than the previous few and, even though I managed to overlook those qualities—just like my other girlfriends, she needed her "independence" and was unable to commit to a relationship.

I have always been drawn to psychics. They're quick, to the point, and they often offer deep insights without having to spend months on the kind of long-winded probing therapists favor. Over the years I've had many sessions with clairvoyants who were spot on, helping to guide me. Of course, I've also seen just as many kooks, like the effeminate, bleached-blond man in his fifties who, throughout my reading, held on his lap a blind chihuahua wearing a tiny sombrero. Swear. Every time the psychic began a sentence—"There's someone coming into your life whose name begins with a T . . ."—the sightless Mexican pooch would squirm and yelp, whereupon the psychic would harshly reprimand him, "Settle down, Pepe, *settle down!*" And there was the woman who, during our session, kept answering her phone, placing bets with her bookie. After the sixth call she finally shrugged apologetically and said, "What can I do? I've got the gift." And I'll never forget the psychic/astrological reading during which the astrologer kept referring to me as a "*Lie*-bra" rather than a "*Lee*-bra." Yeah, I could really focus on what *she* had to say. But even the kooks won me over because each of them had at least one enlightening morsel to offer.

My friend Mark told me he had had a mind-blowing, life-altering reading with a psychic in Van Nuys whose premonitions had convinced him to go to an audition he'd planned to blow off, and there he won a guest-starring role on *Knots Landing*. This woman was no storefront scam artist, Mark assured me—her regulars included a who's who list of Hollywood celebrities.

So I made an appointment to see Madame Zola, Psychic to the Stars.

At the time it seemed like a good idea, but now, sitting in her unventilated living room full of plastic-covered furniture, I'm feeling wary. Tom Selleck and Shelley Long are nowhere in sight. Finally, though, I recognize the familiar brunette in the rocking chair. She could *sort of* pass for a celebrity. She appears on television nightly—hawking goods on the Home Shopping Network. Just a week earlier, during one of my sleepless nights where I was up worrying, it was this very same woman who had almost convinced me to order a set of eight Watering Can Napkin Holders, even though I don't own a single linen napkin.

The plump woman beside me sucks hard on her Lifesaver and shouts at the soap opera on the TV. "Crook!" she cries. I edge away when she begins to bounce excitedly up and down, each bounce unsticking the plastic from her bare, sweaty thighs with a THWAP.

"You watch out or he's gonna get you!" THWAP.

"Don't go with him!" THWAP.

I consider getting up to leave, but I stop myself. I'm desperate. There is so much I need to know. *What else could I write if not movies? I can't sit all day and night in an office so TV staff writing is out, and I don't think I could make a living composing poetry. A book could be great, but what would I write about? And what about my relationships? Will I ever meet anyone who's right for me? And will she stick around?*

I have to stop being so preoccupied with my life. I look around the living room for a distraction and zero in on Madame Zola's elephant collection. First I count them—two on the mirror, five on the mantle, six on the coffee table, four hanging on the wall. Then I break them down into properties—three ivory, four brass, two wooden, three ceramic, five glass. Twenty minutes later, while the Home Shopping Network hawker shifts uncomfortably on her crackling plastic-covered chair, another hefty Eastern European woman saunters into the room from the back of the house. She's wearing a floral-print housedress with furry pink slippers, and sports a terrible cough.

Madame Zola, Psychic to the Stars.

She hacks, and then, with an accent as thick as the fur on her slippers, says, "Stephanie, I ready for Stephanie."

Home Shopping Network lady rises and follows Madame Zola into the back. To avoid obsessing about my situation any further, I begin to count once more. Buttons on the couch under the plastic (twenty-one), pictures of Mary with Baby Jesus (nine), artificial plants (seven). Then I watch the woman next to me jump up and scream at the TV again.

"You're so full of it!" THWAP.

"Stop lying!" THWAP.

I see she's yelling at an Aquafresh commercial.

Finally HSN's Stephanie leaves out the front door, and Madame Zola summons me. I follow her into the kitchen. She stops at a Formica table covered with orange peels and a spray bottle of Lime-A-Way. With a long, loud slurp, Madame Zola swallows a section of an orange and drops heavily into a stained velvet armchair.

"Seet," she says.

I seet on the metal folding chair across from her.

"Geeve me your hand." Madame Zola covers her mouth as she coughs, and then, with that hand, also sticky with orange juice, she grabs mine.

"You tired, no?"

My eyes are dark-circled from lack of sleep—it didn't take a psychic to see that. "Yes, I am," I say, unimpressed.

Cough, cough, cough. "I see relief."

I hope you can say the same for yourself, Sister.

"You have doubts about something?"

"Sure." *Well, she's right about that. That something would be her.*

"I knew that." Cough, cough, cough.

She pulls a Kleenex from a plaid print box and hacks something into the tissue. *Would she have done that if Barbra Streisand were sitting here? Probably. And Babs would rave about her reading, "She was so refreshing. Who feels comfortable enough to expel phlegm in front of me, know what I mean?"*

Madame Zola tosses the soggy tissue into a woven trash basket that brims with previous wads. Her focus returns to me. "I see much confusion."

I perk up. "Yes. That's true. Tell me more, Madame Zola."

"I see a man. Deep, brown eyes. Mysterious."

"Hmmm . . . are you sure it's a man?"

"I see a moustache, you figure," she shrugs. Cough, cough, cough.

Madame Zola, if you know so damn much, why don't you get a fucking lozenge?

"You think too much."

I sit there quietly, thinking about what she has just said.

"You so busy thinking, you no can hear."

I think about that, too.

"Think with heart instead of head. Answers will come." Cough, cough, cough.

For the next fifteen minutes, Madame Zola hacks and tells me many inconsequential things—"You will go on trip someday, somewhere." "Blue is good color for you." "Beware of a Leo." Then she stands up abruptly, hand outstretched.

"Fifty dollar please."

I place the cash on the table, avoiding her coughed-on, sticky hand. I thank Madame Zola and quickly leave her house.

Heading south on the Hollywood Freeway, twisting past Universal Studios, I ponder Madame Zola's words. *"Think with heart instead of head. Cough, cough, cough."*

That night I go to Aviva Center, where I've been volunteering, teaching creative writing. My class is made up of eight teenage girls who represent four races, five gangs, and nine felonies. Uncommunicative at best, they are guarded, hostile, defensive, and defiant. One girl in particular stands out. Raging and rebellious, she constantly speaks of morbidity, destruction, and death. Ironically, her name is Serenity. For the past month she has refused to participate in any writing exercises. But tonight Serenity pulls me aside.

"Here," she says, shoving a pile of her journals into my hands.

"Take 'em. Read 'em. Lemme know what ya think."

When I return home after class, I turn on the TV, keeping the volume low, and then listen to my messages. There's one from my agent regarding a meeting with Disney about a job rewriting a script. *Do I want to rewrite someone else's script? Do I want to write scripts at all? What should I be doing now? Should I even go to the meeting?*

Then, like a spiritual sign reminding me to quiet down and stop spinning out, I see a familiar face on the TV. It's Stephanie on the Home Shopping Network selling a Scrapbook Set by Pixie Press.

I settle onto my bed, open Serenity's journals, and start to read. Piece after piece, in poems and essays and journal entries, her writing is eloquent and powerful, insightful and raw. I'm completely blown away. Her work reminds me of what I love about writing: the art of it, the essence; bold, intimate sharings of soul spilling onto paper what we might not dare say aloud. The kind of writing that has nothing to do with bidding wars and green lights and notes from studio executives' maids.

I get up and stroll outside to my balcony. I see cars snaking in all different directions on the streets below. I breathe in the night-blooming jasmine and listen. Other than a few crickets chirping, it's finally quiet. And—as if illuminated by a spotlight circling the Hollywood skies to announce a premiere—amid the many roads, I clearly see which one to take. Serenity should have a forum for her writing. So should Lakeisha, who's been on the street since she was twelve, and Sara, a chubby, pierced Riot Grrrl who publishes her own zine of rants called *Sourpuss*. Why not write a book and include their voices?

I look up to the Moon, which has always been a comfort since my own teenage days when I hung out on my roof. I feel grateful. Especially to Madame Zola for her sage advice.

And anytime in the future that I find myself thinking with my head instead of my heart, I will give myself a reminder—a simple "Cough, cough, cough."

¡¡ MAC IAREN AAII

THOUGHTS X $\oplus$ BX ① 3/25/91

FALLING, FALLING DEEP INTO DESPAIR
LOOKING AT THE BLOOD PAINTED AIR
I SEE THEM LOOKING AT ME SOLEMLY & STURN
I CRY & CRINGE AS THEY START TO! BURN
"OH" THIS' HORID & DISTORTED ~~~~~ ENDLESS DREAM
I WANT TO JUMP OFF THIS BRIDGE, BUT THERE'S
ONLY A STREAM
MY EYES DON'T SEE THE COLOR'S OF JOY
I FEEL LIKE SOME REJECT OF A HAZORDOUS TOY
MY MIND IS FILLED WITH ONLY EVIL & MORBID THOUGHTS
I'M LOOSING CONTROL & LOOSING A WAR' THAT CAN NOT
RE FOUGHT
I LOOK TO THE SOUTH OF THE HORIZON NOT YET SET
I SEE NOTHING EXCEPT FOR THE NUCLEAR
FALLOUT NOT YET MET.
I DREAM OF UNPURE & HOLY VISIONS
I WAS BORN TO COMPLETE MY SELF DESTRUCTIVE MISSION

Dby Serenity X
Dbi Serenity X
roleamino Parntro

1991

✳ Just weeks after I see *The Silence of the Lambs* I'm in a public sauna when Jodie Foster walks in. Despite already sweating for twenty minutes, I stay an additional half hour and nearly suffer from heat stroke just to watch Jodie talk to her friend. Completely naked.

✳ Rodney King is severely beaten by police officers after leading them on a high-speed chase and resisting arrest. The beating is captured on video and aired repeatedly on television.

✳ I have a garage sale at my house with my friend Daryl Hannah, who makes a *Splash* selling her junk for the first time. I buy some of her used books for a dollar while my old tennis shoes, which she purchases for fifty cents, end up on her feet in *Steel Magnolias*.

✳ Iraq declares some of its chemical weapons and materials to the UN and claims that it does not have a biological weapons program.

✳ Author Douglas Coupland coins the phrase "Generation X" as grunge music hits the scene.

✳ Two of my rerun icons—Natalie Schafer (Lovey on *Gilligan's Island*) and Nancy Kulp (Jane Hathaway on *The Beverly Hillbillies*)—die.

✻ I drive to see 1,760 yellow umbrellas erected near Interstate 5 by the artist Christo, while 1,340 blue umbrellas are simultaneously unfurled in a valley in Japan.

✻ Janet Jackson signs a $30 million contract with Virgin Records, Michael Jackson signs a $65 million contract with Sony, and I receive a $12.43 ASCAP royalty check for my Angel and the Reruns song, "Buffy Come Back," playing on the radio in Thailand, Belgium, and Czechoslovakia.

✻ Michael Landon is treated for cancer and spends weeks in the hospital room next to my father's.

Life, Death, and
My Soap Opera Girlfriend

I met her and fell in love with her as she was dying of leukemia. Well, *she* wasn't—the character she played on a highly rated soap opera was.

She had starred on the show for many years but due to the fact that she wanted to pursue opportunities in feature films, she suddenly contracted the deadly disease and was on her deathbed.

My father had been battling the same deadly disease for three years.

I had never watched a soap opera until I started dating Jennifer. In her final days on the show, her lush blond hair and bright blue eyes couldn't have been more alluring as she gasped, collapsed, and wept in her husband's arms—making him promise he'd move on without her. Even as she was dying, she was radiant.

I can't say the same for my father.

* * *

The blood leaves my arm, flowing swiftly down a tube, passing through a machine, then returning to a vein, this time in my other arm. Since it is accompanied by a torrent of cleansing liquids and hydrating fluids, within moments my bladder is full, and I have to pee like crazy. But I'm stuck in this position and will be for another four hours, needles and tubes in both arms acting as restraints.

If my own father can lie there, being poked and prodded daily, if he can lose his hair and all that he eats; if he can lose his strength, his pride, and any dignity that's left as a nurse has to clean the bed he has soiled; if he can barely open his eyes but still make jokes and make sure the nurses don't feel put out; then I can lie here restrained, with blood and liquids flowing, bladder bursting, as the technicians collect platelets that could very well save Dad's life—for the moment, at least.

*　　*　　*

The first time Jennifer and I kissed, we were at her memorial service. It was held in a friend's backyard one late summer afternoon, and everyone came dressed in black and delivered eulogies honoring her dead character, Emily Stevenson.*

They spoke of her boldness, her beauty; her youth and her restlessness—all the days of her life—keeping up the ruse late into the evening. I even made a donation to the Leukemia Society in memory of her character.

As Jennifer and I began to see each other regularly, something happened that I never expected. I got hooked. Not just on Jennifer, but on her soap opera. It didn't matter that she was dead and gone; the characters continued to speak of her, mourn her, and have flashbacks of her, so I still felt her presence. And by the time they stopped mentioning her altogether, it was too late for me. I had developed a serious habit.

This was not exactly the best time to start a new romance. For the previous three years I had been taking care of my father while he was in and out of the hospital. I had spent every day by his side while my mother was relegated to keeping their business running, and, although my brother was frequently at the hospital donating platelets

---

* Jennifer's name and the character she played have been changed.

for my dad, he was mostly busy struggling to support his family and raise two young children. Since I was now writing a book and made my own hours, I was able to do my work as I kept my dad company, massaged his feet, ran to summon the nurse, and questioned the doctors.

*　　*　　*

"Squeeze my hand," I say. I hold on to him, tightly.

"Oh, sorry, Bob," the nurse keeps repeating. "I'm so sorry." She continually pokes my father's arm with a large needle, trying to put in a new IV.

Charming and still handsome at sixty-four, with the face of a seasoned character actor who could have played the kindly neighbor, my father is beloved by all the nurses.

"Let's try it again," she says. She inserts the needle into another vein.

My strong, unshakable dad winces and squeezes my hand until it's numb. Pools of blood form under his skin, instantly bruising.

"Sorry, Bob. You have no veins left, and the couple I see just keep rolling," she tries to explain as she pokes once more, creating another clotting mass.

Finally my dad loosens his grip around my hand and focuses all his attention on the nurse.

"Good thing I kicked that heroin habit," he teases.

She laughs, eases up. The IV needle finally settles into a vein.

*　　*　　*

One evening, about six months after Jennifer and I began seeing each other, I arrived at her house and found her on the doorstep talking to a striking woman who looked like she had stepped out of the pages of a European *Vogue*.

"Hey, I want you to meet Vincenza," Jennifer said. "She's my international agent. Vincenza, this is my girlfriend, Hillary."

"Nice to meet you," we both said, shaking hands.

"Guess what, Honey? We're going to Rome."

"You are? That's great. When do you guys leave?"

"No, *we* are going. You and I."

"What?"

"*Jjjjjhyes*," Vincenza said, drawing out the word in her thick Italian accent. "Jennifer we want for magazine photos spread. She huge star in Italy. It shoot in Rome next week for three weeks, and she only come if you come. I say jjjjjjhyes."

"Wow," was about all I could utter.

I had never been to Europe and had always dreamed of going. And what a way to go. Star treatment, all expenses paid, in the throes of a wild romance. It was perfect. Except for one small detail.

I didn't want to leave my dad.

*   *   *

There is a specific smell on the third floor cancer ward of Saint John's Hospital that wafts into the elevator doors as soon as they open. Sour and foul, perhaps it's the closest thing to the scent of death.

A therapist tells me to shield myself before going into the hospital. Every day I stop before the doors that slide open to the lobby, and there I take a deep breath of what seems like fresh air, even in Los Angeles. I visualize a shield around me, protecting my body, heart, and soul, but I make it a glass one so I'm not shutting out anything I need to receive or, more important, give.

*   *   *

When the trip came up, my father's leukemia was in remission. He hadn't been in the hospital or on chemo for several months. He had even returned to work. I told him about Rome, and he said, "Of course you're going. End of discussion."

"What if something happens to you while I'm gone? I'd never forgive myself."

Hillary Carlip

"If you stay here on my account and miss this opportunity, *I'll* never forgive you, so either way you're screwed."

In fact, my dad announced, during the time I would be away, he was going to Dallas on a business trip. So off Jennifer and I went to Italy.

Upon our arrival, a limo picked us up at the airport, and we sped down the streets, an incongruous sight—flashy car among ancient ruins. In media-glutted Los Angeles, Jennifer was rarely recognized. Though I had heard that she was internationally famous, her face even plastered on potato chip bags in Greece, neither one of us was prepared for what was about to happen.

As we neared the hotel, we saw an enormous crowd waiting outside. When the limo pulled up and they spotted Jennifer, the entire mob surrounded us, screaming and knocking on the windows. Homemade signs read: "Jennifer we love!" and "Welcome Emily Stevenson to Roma!"

"No way," was all Jennifer could say.

"Jjjjjhyes way," I teased as we pried our way out of the car. Jennifer was rushed by the throng who shouted out praise in Italian and begged for her autograph. Paparazzi cameras flashed.

About an hour later we finally managed to reach our room. Inside the luxurious digs, Jennifer grabbed me in her arms and led me to the bed. But I stopped her. "I have to do one thing first."

I called my dad.

*   *   *

One day, several months prior to Rome, we are in the outpatient area on the second floor at Saint John's. Dad's been home from the hospital for a week, but I still take him there every other day for either chemo or blood and platelet transfusions. Even though my father has lost twenty pounds, all of his hair, and most of his strength, he won't allow his spirits to weaken. He brings the nurses candy, and they all fawn over him.

I hold it together like I never have before. I am normally someone whose emotions are so irrepressible, when it comes to crying I often don't have a say in the matter. Once when I was watching *The Price Is Right* a woman whose bra strap stuck out from her sleeveless top won the big showcase, and as she jumped in excitement, her wig slid down, forcing her to adjust it on national television. I cried for ten minutes. But now I need to be strong for my father—as brave as he's being. As he sits there, blood emptying from a hanging pouch into his veins, I ask, "Can I go to the cafeteria and get you anything?"

"Nah, I'm okay," he answers.

"Come on, they've got some good-lookin' desserts down there. How about some ice cream or chocolate cake?" The love-of-sweets gene runs deep in my family.

And then my dad looks up at me with, I swear, a twinkle in his eyes and a devilish, childlike smile—he looks like he's about five years old. "I'll have a strawberry ice cream cone."

"Perfect. I'll be right back."

And that's all it takes. I make it out to the hallway and walk slowly to the elevator, sobbing in soundless convulsions, nose dripping, eyes overflowing. I continue crying all the way down to the basement floor cafeteria. In the hallway, I pause to sit on a bench in front of a statue of a saint. I read the descriptive plaque beneath it: St. Dimpna, Patron Saint of Family Happiness. Sure.

I return to the transfusion room, having pulled myself together. I watch my father—my rock—eat a strawberry ice cream cone with one hand while the other stays motionless, red blood dripping into withered vein; I see the pink ice cream glistening on his upper lip and chin. And as I wipe his face, there in front of him for the first time, I start to weep.

*   *   *

Jennifer and I spent every morning in Rome together, falling again and again onto the floor through the crack in our pushed-together twin beds. We'd kiss good-bye with the windows wide open but the blinds still closed, just to make sure none of her fans, who were gathered in the streets below, repeatedly chanting her name, would spot us.

On her way out of the hotel lobby, Jennifer would stop to sign autographs, pose for pictures, accept gifts and flowers, then push through the crowd to her waiting limo, which would whisk her away to that day's location. I sometimes joined her, but more often I wandered on my own, exploring. With exquisite shrines on just about every street corner and elaborate statues and fountains at each turn, the city transported me. I wandered from piazza to palazzo, sat in outdoor cafes in front of ancient monuments, and was mesmerized by backstreets, saints, cathedral bells, and painters working at easels. I never once stopped thinking of my father. I'd meditate and visualize him healthy and well; I'd visit churches and light candles for him.

At dusk I waited in our hotel room for Jennifer. The smell of tulips, roses, garlic, and burning myrrh filled the room from the streets, accompanied by shadows and light and the sound of honking horns and footsteps on cobblestone.

We dined in outdoor restaurants, sharing romantic dinners under twinkling white lights snaking through overhanging branches. We were always being watched, so in public we didn't touch. But that only fueled our connection, intensified our desire, so by nightfall, when we returned to our hotel room and closed the blinds, allowing in only a sliver of moonlight, we held back nothing. Although Europe had always seemed far away and foreign, now it felt so familiar. And no matter how far from home I was, there was that same Moon, shining her light and grace down on us.

*   *   *

"Can I get you anything?" I ask my dad as he squirms with pain in his hospital bed.

"A gun," he jokes, with as much strength as he can muster.

"Sorry, mine didn't get through the metal detector downstairs. How about I read to you instead?"

"Sure."

I've just been to the Bodhi Tree, where I bought several books about healing, about focus and will—about miracles.

My father is an artist. Although he stopped painting and sculpting early on in my life, reminders fill my parents' house. Easels and palettes with crusty oil globs still smelling of color are tucked into closets; the dining room floor he carved and stained in an elaborate pattern remains; the table with a large sundial on top that he made is the centerpiece of the den, where the shutters with ancient Egyptian scenarios that he carved two decades earlier still cover the windows.

But by the time I reached my twenties, Dad was increasingly consumed by his business—the juvenile furniture manufacturing and distributing company he took over from his father—and he stopped painting, creating, or expressing. He was up at 5:00 a.m., out the door and to the office before 7:00; he returned home in time for dinner with the family, a nightly ritual consisting of my brother and me arguing, invariably ending with my father yelling, "Can't I please have some quiet?" Then he'd head up to bed and stay there until the next day when he was off again to work. He had settled into a routine so precise that every morning before he left, he checked for five things: his upper shirt pocket for his glasses, his back pants pocket for his wallet, his front left pocket for his keys, right pocket for his lighter, and left jacket pocket for his cigarettes.

I decide to read to him from a book by Louise Hay called *You Can Heal Your Life*.

"Oh this is interesting, there's a list of Probable Mental Patterns that cause specific illnesses. Should I see what mental pattern causes leukemia?"

"I'm not so sure I want to know," my dad says. "Ah, why not, go ahead."

I find leukemia and am stunned into silence.

Hillary Carlip

"So?"

Those damn tears start to flow again. I turn away so he doesn't see as they spill right onto the page.

"Come on, I can take it," my dad prods.

I'm not so sure he can.

But I wipe my tears, pull myself together, then turn back to read the cause aloud to him.

"Leukemia: Brutally killing inspiration.'"

*   *   *

In Rome I wandered into almost every church. Surrounded by ancient paintings, mosaics, gold leaf, statues, and altars lit with candles placed by those asking for and receiving, I melted into God's presence. I prayed that I would never do what my father had done. I vowed to continually nurture my creativity, to keep my inspiration alive and burning as brightly as the flame-lit altars.

On the day my father was to return to L.A. from Dallas I woke up at 4:00 a.m. and quietly tiptoed downstairs to a pay phone in the lobby of our hotel. With the time difference, my father would have just arrived home from the airport. Instead I heard my brother's voice answer my parents' phone. He hesitantly told me Dad had gone back to the hospital. On his return trip he felt so much pain in his legs that he had to ask for a wheelchair to transport him from the airplane's gate. My father was a man who always had everything together, and when he didn't, he had to appear as if he did. For him to ask for a wheelchair—this was serious.

I called the hospital.

"I'm coming home today," I declared, when my mom answered the phone. I heard her hand the receiver over.

"No you are not," my dad replied firmly. "I'm fine."

"You're not fine, you're in the hospital—you had to get a wheelchair at the airport. That is not fine."

"Look, I'm not going to die now. I promise. All you've been doing is taking care of me. Please, Hill, just stay and enjoy yourself. Honestly, that's what would make me feel best."

I hung up and walked back to our room. I climbed into bed, and as Jennifer took me in her arms I began to cry.

"Come on, Honey, let it all out," she whispered, holding me safely.

And I did, sobbing for hours, finally releasing the torrents that had been stuck deep in my soul, gnawing at my skin.

There in a hotel room in Rome, I surrendered.

*   *   *

My mom works all day, then at about 5:00 comes to relieve me at the hospital. She tells me she does her crying at the office, slipping into the bathroom or taking a walk outside, and also at night, home alone in the bed she has been sharing with my father for forty years. Since I returned from Rome, I can no longer hold back.

"Dad, I've been trying to be all strong for you, but you know what?"

"What?"

"This sucks. Of course I'm a wreck—how could I not be? So from here on in, you're just gonna have to deal with me crying."

The tears fall now, with no restraint. My father sees and takes my hand.

"You know what?" he echoes my query, his voice shaky.

"What?"

"You're right. This does suck."

Then, for the first time since he got sick four years ago, my father starts to cry.

*   *   *

By the time we returned from Rome, Jennifer's widower had already remarried. I knew because I watched the soap every afternoon, as soon as I came home from the hospital. It helped me unwind.

Hillary Carlip

On the Fourth of July, Jennifer and I planned to go to a barbecue at a friend's house. On the way, we stopped by the hospital to visit my dad. He cracked jokes, trying his damndest to be as charming as always, despite his pain. We all laughed and hugged; he shooed us out, encouraging us to go have some fun. Hours later, while at the barbecue, I received a call from my mother—my dad had taken a turn for the worse, and suddenly he was in and out of consciousness. We raced back to the hospital.

*   *   *

"You should gather the family," the doctor informs us. It could be today or tomorrow."

Doctors never use the words "die" or "death." They talk around it. At this moment, I am grateful. Death is still a distant notion, vague and surreal.

We gather close friends and family—including my dad's parents, who can't fathom that they are going to outlive their sixty-four-year-old son. We hold a constant vigil at his bedside. My dad—the fighter, the trooper—remains feisty. The doctor's prediction, "today or to-morrow," does not arrive. One day, two days, three days, four.

Jennifer, who stays by my side all these days, walks with me down the third-floor hallway. We both need to take a breath. Her arm is around me; we're not saying a word. Nothing makes a person more present than imminent death. As we stroll, we almost collide with a middle-aged woman on one of those hall walks that every visitor to the cancer ward takes at one time or another. She looks up, startled.

"Oh my God, it's you."

We stare at her, not understanding.

"Emily Stevenson. You're alive."

Before Jennifer can respond, the woman adds, "I mean I know you're the actress and all, but, oh my God—my mother and I watched you every single day. She's been sick for a long time now."

It's getting harder for me to breathe, almost suffocated by someone else's pain on top of my own.

"I know this sounds crazy, but my mom isn't doing so well. Maybe if you could come to her room and say hello, you know, show her you're really alive, maybe it would help."

"Of course, I'd be happy to," Jennifer smiles compassionately.

We follow the woman with messy salt-and-pepper hair towards the room where her mother lies, dying. I wait outside the door and watch as Jennifer enters the room. I see the mother, tubes in her arms, oxygen mask on her face, lying motionless. I don't hear what they say to each other, but I see my girlfriend take this woman's hand in hers, and I see the life force returning. A glimmer comes to the woman's eye, a smile on her dry, cracked lips. And then she gathers all the strength that's in her, sits up, and hugs Jennifer. They hug for a long time.

On day five of our vigil, Jennifer has to leave to go to an important audition. Soon afterward she returns to the hospital, looking even more gorgeous than usual. She's wearing a tight, short skirt, heels, a cleavage-revealing blouse, and her hair and makeup are impeccable.

My father, who has not spoken for days as he drifts between worlds, continually gasping what could be his last breath, notices her walk into the room. He slowly turns his head and through his partially opened eyes, gets a good look at Jennifer. Inspired by her beauty, he utters his final word before he dies an hour later.

My father just says, "WOW."

YOU ARE THE BEST!

WITH
LOVE
by
3 twins sister's
Bina Tatiana Renata

A card that came with flowers, given to my soap opera girlfriend by Roman triplets

1993

* The World Wide Web is born. I do my first online chat in preparation for promoting the book I've recently sold, *Girl Power*. Only one other person is in the chat room and we both LOL over the fact. ;)

* Ten years after hanging out with Tom Hanks when my band Angel and the Reruns shot the film *Bachelor Party* with him, he stars in *Philadelphia*, for which he will win the Acadamy Award for best actor.

* Michael Jackson is accused of child molestation but charges are dropped when a settlement agreement is reached. Good thing for him that's over with.

* A bomb goes off at the World Trade Center, killing six people and injuring more than a thousand. Good thing more people weren't killed.

* Weight loss advocate Susan Powter screams from infomercials and books to STOP THE INSANITY!

* Twenty years ago I was given a free ticket to see what would be Barbra Streisand's last concert, at a McGovern for President benefit. Now I am given another free ticket to the event of the year—her comeback performance on New Year's Eve at the MGM Grand in Vegas. Too bad I'm still not really a fan of hers.

* A star-studded year of friends: I spend Christmas Eve with Melissa Etheridge, who comes out at Clinton's inaguration ball; k.d. lang, with Grammy nominations for Album of the Year, Record of the Year, Song of the Year, and Best Female Pop Vocal, comes to my house for dinner and sings her hit song "Constant Craving" in the hallway; and since my good friend's boyfriend is John Cusack, I see him in bed one night wearing acne medicine.

* To gather writing for *Girl Power*, I go to a teen girl wheelchair basketball game, an Indian reservation, a home for teen mothers, and weekly Riot Grrrl Meetings. "Revolution Girl-Style Now!"

* LAPD raids the home of Hollywood Madame Heidi Fleiss, and Lorena Bobbitt cuts off her husband's penis, while Janet Jackson scores a hit with "That's the Way Love Goes."

Vespas, Vespas, All Fall Down

What do you do when you're on a self-imposed sabbatical from serial monogamy and meet the person you'll probably spend the rest of your life with?

Run like hell.

That's exactly what I did when I met Maxine.

When I was involved with Jennifer, my life became much like her soap opera. My father died from a dreaded disease; with no prior experience my mother was forced to take over the family business; my previous two girlfriends, Elizabeth and Katie, fell in love with each other; a close friend miscarried in her eighth month of pregnancy; my housemate, Ken, after a lengthy search, discovered that despite the fact that his birth mother had given him up for adoption in Brooklyn thirty years ago, the two of them had been living just one block from each other in L.A.'s San Fernando Valley until her death one month before he tracked down her identity; and Jennifer plummeted into a deep depression, which she had had previous bouts with during our relationship. Through arduous therapy sessions (mine, not Jennifer's!), I came to realize I had developed a pattern. According to my therapist, darkness was seductive to me since I believed that my own light would nurture, encourage, inspire, and heal my mate, which, in turn, would make me worthy and necessary. That'll be $3,755, please.

Then in a climactic episode, the night before Jennifer and I were to leave on a trip for my birthday—staying in intimate bed and breakfasts throughout New England to watch the leaves turn color—I went to sleep on "my" side of Jennifer's bed and on "my" nightstand I found bobby pins. Jennifer, the soap opera actress, gave a Daytime Emmy-worthy performance, swearing she had no idea how they had gotten there. But I, the amateur detective, not only knew exactly how they had, but also whose they were. Come on, who the hell wears bobby pins?

We still went to see the leaves turn color except what turned the most throughout our trip was my stomach, especially when Jennifer would go off to make a "work" phone call. Yeah, to her bobby pin-wearing "agent" no doubt.

In a romantic bed and breakfast overlooking an orange-and-red maple forest, I decided that the best birthday gift I could give myself was a break from relationships. And more than just a commercial break—it was time for a hiatus.

I spent the first few months of my time off mostly in tears, mourning the loss of my father, of Jennifer, and of all my failed relationships. But by mid-spring I started getting into a groove and actually began to really enjoy my freedom. I was hanging out daily with Wendy and Lisa from Prince and the Revolution, having officially made the leap from fan to close friend (*really* this time!), and felt more creative than I had in years. I was feverishly working on my book *Girl Power* and, vowing not to squelch inspiration as my father had, I began to make visual art—found object assemblages—and showing and selling pieces in established galleries. I took all the energy I had been giving to my girlfriends and instead infused it into my work and my life.

By fall, I was celebrating one exciting, powerful year of being on my own.

And then I met Maxine.

Hillary Carlip

Katie, my ex who had remained a close friend, had gone out with Maxine a few times, but on each date, she said, she kept thinking that Maxine and *I* should meet. "We'll all go out to dinner," she announced. "You have to know each other, you'd be perfect together."

That's precisely why I kept putting off the dinner. "I'm not ready for a relationship now," I declared. "I'm loving being alone."

Katie finally convinced me to go out with her and Maxine on a chilly Thursday night in November. We met at Pane e Vino, an intimate Italian restaurant on Beverly. Maxine was charming and adorable, funny and smart. (Damn.) She was a TV writer-producer working on the number-one hit sitcom, so she was also creative and successful. (Crap.) And then she invited Katie and me to a screening the following night of Catherine Deneuve's new film, *Indochine*, premiering at an event Maxine was producing to benefit Amnesty International—she had a conscience, too. (Shit.)

After dinner, we went to her house, a big mistake for someone trying to avoid a relationship, because her home was as intriguing and inviting as Maxine. A bungalow near the Hollywood Bowl, every room was splashed with colors deep and bright, walls filled with brilliant art—similar to the kind I had been making. In a corner of the red-and-yellow living room sat a drum set, one bass drum with "SAMMY" across it, the other emblazoned with "DAVIS JR." "Sammy was the greatest entertainer of all time," she said, "and when his estate was being auctioned off, I had to rescue his drum kit." She told me she was a performer—she used to do stand-up comedy and even had a band—then turned to writing. She had a deep love of variety shows since childhood, so she completely freaked when I confessed I had been a juggler and fire-eater. She even had a very specific collection of old tiki bowls and mugs from Harvey's, a restaurant in Lake Tahoe in the fifties and sixties. I too had collected Harvey's bowls.

All of this did not bode well.

That night Maxine asked me to dinner for the following week. I hesitated. Besides my resistance to what seemed inevitable, another quality about Maxine made me nervous. She was so upbeat and optimistic. Maxine had her *own* light—she didn't need mine. However, I did agree to see her.

On the morning of what was to be our first date, Maxine called. "Wanna go to breakfast so we can discuss where we're gonna go for dinner?" she asked.

Amusing and charming, right? But her enthusiasm freaked me out. Here was someone I wouldn't be able to just "date." When Maxine and I did take the plunge, it was obvious we'd be together for years to come. And I just wasn't ready for that. But would I ever be? Suddenly it dawned on me that maybe *I* was the one with the commitment problem. Perhaps that's why I always chose others who couldn't commit—to let *me* off the hook. Hell, I couldn't even commit to one career, afraid I might be missing out on something else.

And, despite the pull, I found plenty more reasons for not getting involved with Maxine. If I was showered with the kind of attention and care that I'd never really before received, could I give up being so self-reliant? What would I *do* in a relationship with a person who had nothing to "fix"? Could I stand giving my heart to someone and risk having them carelessly neglect it again? Could I take any more loss so soon after losing my dad?

I couldn't start seeing Maxine but I also couldn't *not* see her. I passed on breakfast but did keep our plans for dinner.

During our first couple of weeks of "dating," I tried to take it slow. In fact, I was always putting on the brakes. Maxine would call me four times a day; I'd call back once. One day she sang "I've Got the World on a String" in its entirety on my answering machine, each verse ending in "I'm in love." I had to stop seeing her for an entire week after that. We'd sleep together only on weekends—luckily she was busy working so she didn't have that many nights available anyway. When we did hang out, we always had a great time. On Sundays we'd wake at 5:00 a.m., make coffee, and head into the chilly winter mornings combing the flea markets, sharing the steamy, caffeinated

brew from a little red thermos cup as we searched for vintage trea-
sures. We went to Outsider Art exhibits at museums and hung out
with each other's fascinating friends and equally fascinating exes who
had become family.

But then came spring and with it a hiatus from her TV show.
Maxine wanted to go to Europe. And she wanted to take me with her.
I still had plenty of issues with receiving—the last trip to Europe was
paid for by Jennifer's job, not *her*. Letting Maxine pay would be tough,
and since I wasn't making enough money to afford the trip, that was
the only option. I also was definitely not ready to be with her—hell,
anyone—twenty-four hours a day, seven days a week, for three whole
weeks. But she persisted, and despite my trepidation, I agreed to go.

On a cool day in May we flew to Paris. The more romantic Maxine
was, the more I stiffened in terror. So we argued while eating lavender
crème brûlée in Juan-les-Pins, sobbed during a boat ride in the Blue
Grotto on Capri, broke up in a sacred forest in the south of France,
and didn't speak a word to each other in a sleeping car train to Posi-
tano. We had heavy discussions about our relationship at three ancient ruins, two seashores, in four taxis, and at six outdoor cafés. Poor
Maxine was mystified.

Finally we decided to cancel the last leg of our trip, Venice, and go
home early instead. We took a train to Rome, where we would spend
our final night before flying back to L.A. Now that the pressure was
off, we didn't argue; we didn't even weep. We rented Vespa scooters
and tooled around town. At twilight we rode to a charming outdoor
café on the Piazza Navona. Other patrons had parked their scooters out front, lined up in a row like a Vespa showroom. So I gave my
scooter a little gas and picked up the front wheel a bit to ride up on
the curb and join them.

I pulled to the end of the row and parked next to the last scooter,
then watched as Maxine gave her scooter a little gas and turned to pull
up onto the curb. Not enough gas. She tried again, but this time gave
it a bit more throttle than necessary. Suddenly Maxine was careening

full speed ahead, doing an unintentional wheelie right in front of a statue of Jesus. As she tried to slow down, her scooter peeled out of control, wiped out, and slammed into the scooter parked at the top of the row. That scooter banged into the next parked scooter which thwacked the next, and the next, and the next, and the next. As I stood and stared in stunned silence, each Vespa fell, like dominoes, until, at last, my scooter went down, and *I* was knocked to the ground, under the whole pile.

Maxine's pants were ripped, her knee and arm bloodied, and both of us lay sprawled on the sidewalk. We looked up at each other and simultaneously said, "Are you okay?" We each nodded. Then we burst out laughing. Uncontrollably. We laughed so hard that despite the pain and the fact that we still couldn't stand up yet, it was our cheeks that hurt most. It was a relief to feel pain somewhere other than in our hearts.

When we finally stopped laughing I looked at the mess we'd made and saw each fallen scooter as a symbol of each of my reasons for not allowing myself to be in this relationship: "I can't take so much attention"; "I'm scared to commit"; "I can't handle being with someone so together, someone who doesn't need my help"; "It's too soon after Dad died, I can't handle any more potential loss."

One by one each of my excuses was knocked to the ground.

And there I lay, under the pile, scratched and scarred but still in one piece.

I picked myself up, limped over to help Maxine, and surrendered to the destiny I had been trying so desperately to avoid.

We never did make it to Venice. But we did manage to make it to each other.

SCOOTERS FOR RENT
Via della Purificazione 84 · ROME ☎ 4885485
Near Piazza Barberini

1997, 1998, 1999

1997

❋ As breaking news follows alleged murderer O. J. Simpson driving to the courthouse for the verdict in the civil case against him, I spot my girlfriend Maxine on TV, on her way to a meeting, coincidentally *driving behind O.J.*

❋ We get season ticket courtside seats to the premiere year of the WNBA. At every game we sit next to L.A. Sparks player Lisa Leslie's mom and failed O.J. prosecutor Christopher Darden.

❋ Princess Di is killed in a tragic accident as her car tries to elude paparazzi.

❋ Maya Angelou's memoir, *I Know Why the Caged Bird Sings,* is banned from the ninth-grade English curriculum in Maryland because some horrible, nasty, stupid white parents say it "portrays white people as being horrible, nasty, stupid people."

❋ While promoting my book, *Girl Power*, I speak at Wellesley College. Meanwhile, Wellesley graduate Hillary Rodham Clinton doesn't have a clue that her husband Bill is spilling his semen on White House intern Monica Lewinsky's navy blue dress.

✳ Two years after my book is released, the hugely successful Spice Girls sell over 45 million albums and make a mockery of, I mean *popularize*, the term Girl Power.

1998

✳ Smoking is banned in all California bars and restaurants. Good thing my father died because of his smoking habit and didn't have to live to see this day.

✳ Fifty-five-year-old Michael Douglas's divorce is final, leaving him free to be with his girlfriend Catherine Zeta-Jones, twenty-five years his junior. FDA approves Viagra for use as a treatment for male impotence.

✳ I play basketball every Sunday with a group of female friends and several "celebrity guests" who stop by and play with us, including Rosie O'Donnell, Martina Navratilova, Sara Gilbert, and Melissa Etheridge.

✳ Just months after President Clinton denies he had sexual relations with "that woman," he admits in taped testimony that he indeed did. At the MTV Movie Awards, Jim Carrey wins for his convincing performance in the film *Liar Liar*.

1999

✳ Rev. Jerry Falwell warns parents that since a popular Teletubby carries a purse, is purple, and has an antenna shaped like a triangle, Tinky Winky is gay.

✳ Charlton Heston serves his second year as president of the National Rifle Association as two Littleton, Colorado, teenagers open fire on their teachers and fellow students, killing thirteen and injuring twenty-four at Columbine High School.

* Katie and I collaborate with Debbie Gibson, now Deborah Gibson, to adapt *Skirts* into a Broadway musical. At a reading in our producer's living room, future Tony winner for *Hairspray*, Marissa Jaret Winokur, plays one of the lead roles, and fan-favorite soap opera star Ricky Paull Goldin another.

* Lance Armstrong wins his first Tour de France and, after eighteen failed nominations, Susan Lucci finally wins a Daytime Emmy Award for her role on *All My Children*.

* Maxine and I, along with another partner, start an enormous Internet Company—Voxxy, an online network for teen girls. We get Jennifer Aniston to be our spokesperson and do a broadband show with us, and I go from a life of freelance to being a boss of about forty employees.

* As we head into Y2K, everyone stockpiles supplies and prepares for all the disasters that might occur on New Year's Eve, when the clock strikes midnight.

Leaving Las Vegas . . .
Please!

A word of warning: If you ever say to your mother, "Think about what you'd enjoy doing, just name it, and I'll do it with you," *be prepared*.

Feeling badly about not spending enough time with Mom after my dad died, and seeing how hard she worked to continue running his business, overwhelmed with responsibilities, I mistakenly made that offer. I figured it was the least I could do—go with her to see some theater, join a book club together, go shopping.

But no, my mother wanted me to take her to Hell.

I remember an episode of *Night Gallery* that I saw in the early seventies where John Astin, best known for his classic portrayal of Gomez Addams, the French-spouting, arm-kissing patriarch of the creepy and kooky *Addams Family*, played a hippie who died and was sent to Hell. Only there he found no fiery inferno, no whips or chains, no snake pits or vats of boiling oil. His Hell was a drab room covered in ugly wallpaper, where an elderly suburban couple showed endless slides of their summer vacation—forcing the hippie to face an eternal after-lifetime of boredom.

Had I been featured in that episode, condemned to my own distinct version of Hell, viewers would have been subjected to the sight of me in the most plastic, soulless, hyperoxygenated, boob-inflated, money-sucking place on earth—Las Vegas.

In the *Night Gallery* episode, the devil was quick to point out to the tormented hippie that "Up there, this identical room is someone else's idea of Heaven."

So give the devil his due. For while Vegas is my Hell, it is Mim Carlip's Heaven on Earth.

1997. The first year I took my mom to Vegas (yeah, this became a yearly sojourn of torture), we were sitting in a restaurant at the MGM Grand after a long, tedious day of losing money at the quarter slots. As we were both digging into oversized ninety-nine-cent shrimp cocktails, one of the televisions at the bar showed some headline news.

Mother Teresa had just died.

I closed my eyes to quietly honor the life of the saintly woman who had devoted her years to helping the sick and needy, to spreading compassion and goodness throughout the world. But my contemplation was interrupted by the arrival of an unruly group of drunken "islanders" who gave Gilligan—and the Skipper, too—a run for their money. Dressed in tie-dyed sarongs, fake flowered leis, and Hawaiian shirts that were louder than the inebriated revelers themselves, each of them wore on their head a large, brightly colored felt or velour *stuffed parrot*, beak rising high, tail feathers flowing down necks and backs. As the waitresses served them frothy drinks, the female revelers, wearing bras concocted of coconut halves, began to sloppily sing, "Wastin' away again in Margaritaville. . . ." The men, wearing flip-flops embossed with parrots and sunglasses festooned with the same feathered friend of choice, joined in at full volume. A hugely pregnant woman in a T-shirt with the words "Parakeet Inside" sequined over her belly sang loudest and most out of tune.

Hellooo! Mother Teresa just died, motherfuckers!

I asked our waitress, whose Fu Manchu acrylic nails were dotted with rhinestone flowers, "What's going on?"

"Oh," she answered matter-of-factly. "Those are Parrot Heads."

"Parrot Heads?"

"Jimmy Buffett fans," the waitress explained slowly, as if I had some sort of learning impediment.

There was a huge outburst from the tropical posse as they returned to the chorus of their object of devotion's greatest hit. Not a tinge of solemnity. You could bet that if Jimmy Buffett had gone to that big island in the sky, they'd all be removing their stuffed parrot hats out of respect and crying into their margaritas.

As we left the restaurant, I saw an elderly woman sitting at the Wheel of Fortune slots, weeping. Finally. *Someone's* showing some reverence for Mother Teresa's passing. I smiled at her and asked, "Are you okay?"

She shook her head. "It's terrible. Tragic. I've just been denied a cash advance on my ATM card."

1998. As if something or someone were forcing Mom and me to look Heaven and Hell right in the face, the following year's trek to Vegas featured another icon's demise.

This time the breaking news unfolded while we were staying at the Mirage. I had convinced my girlfriend, Maxine, to join us despite the fact that she hates Vegas as much as I do—especially after doing gigs at most of the hotels during her stand-up comedy days.

At 6:00 a.m. Maxine was still asleep, and Mom had already hit the slots. I was at the hotel gym, running on a treadmill that featured its own built-in television, relieved there was no cardio equipment with built-in slot machines. I turned on CNN and suddenly saw a "death montage." When a series of still pictures of a celebrity's early days flashes on the news, even with the sound off you can tell that the person has met their maker.

This time the celeb happened to be Mr. Las Vegas himself.

Frank Sinatra had just died.

I ran back to the room to tell Maxine. For the next two hours we huddled on the bed watching the coverage, and imagined how the city would pay homage to the Chairman of the Board. Frank's likeness would be carved into butter sculptures at all the $12.99 buffets. In his honor, the Liberace museum would temporarily shroud the world's largest rhinestone. Men would eat ham and eggs off of hooker's boobs like Frank did, according to Kitty Kelley's unauthorized biography. (Were they sunny-side up? That seems redundant with boobs. I would have gone with scrambled or a nice cheese omelet.)

It was time to meet Mom in the lobby so we headed down in the elevator. We gasped when we heard the piped-in music playing "The Lady Is a Tramp" and wondered if it was just a coincidence or if the Muzak programmers had already begun their tributes.

When the elevator doors opened, I was immediately assaulted with all that I hate most about Vegas. A cloud of toxic smoke in the shape of an iron lung hovered above the Pai Gow poker tables. The casino smelled like a nauseating combo-platter of stale beer and White Diamonds, Liz Taylor's perfume, which, years later, would provoke a bus driver to go berserk on an over-scented passenger. I heard buzzers and whistles and bells and sirens, like France during the occupation, and I even saw an old man at a roulette table, smoking a cigarette through the tracheotomy hole in his neck.

Mom was waiting by longtime bachelors Siegfried and Roy's white tigers, on display behind glass. "Did you hear?" I asked.

"Hear what?"

Max broke the news. "Ol' Blue Eyes shut his peepers for good. Frank Sinatra passed away."

My mother gasped. "That's so sad." She welled up with tears and opened her purse to find a Kleenex. "Oh, sorry," she said, embarrassed when she noticed her nicely manicured hands had turned black from the coins she'd been handling all morning. "You girls go ahead to the buffet. I'll wash and meet you there."

My mother caught up with us between the omelet bar and the

make-your-own-waffle station. We piled our plates high with empty carbs and moved to a booth.

"Mom," I said, chewing on a cold, rubbery waffle, which was more of a *wawful*, "don't you think it's kind of weird that whenever we come to Vegas someone famous kicks off?"

She looked up from her oversized, most likely genetically enhanced, corn muffin. "Yeah, it is kind of strange."

"Maybe we'd better stop coming," I declared.

Mom's lower lip jutted out. "Hill, I don't understand what you don't like about Vegas."

Then, in perfect timing, as if they magically appeared just to illustrate my point, Cher, Michael Jackson, President Clinton, and Marilyn Monroe sat down in the booth next to us with plates of eggs benedict.

"Need I say more?" I answered. "Everything's fake here. Even the hotels are busy trying to be something they're not—Egypt, Rome, New York."

Maxine chimed in. "Mim, I understand why you might have loved Vegas years ago—when Frank and Sammy and the rest of the Rat Pack played here—when Ann-Margret rode onto the stage on her motorcycle. But today it's just so. . . ." Her voice trailed off, depleted by the depleted scene around us.

Like a lawyer steadfastly defending her client, Mom inhaled deeply for dramatic effect. Then the words poured out. "I think it's exciting and alive, like nothing in our everyday lives. I love the noise, the energy. Maybe it's the oxygen they pump in, but I always feel high when I'm here. Did you notice there aren't any clocks around? It's timeless . . . mindless. It's like anything goes."

I saw it then and there. For as mundane as her life in L.A. was, in Vegas, Mom's world sparkled. I fell silent.

We spent the rest of the day dropping coins into the slots, my mother chanting in Sinatra's honor, "Luck be a lady!" Per usual, she wasn't.

Then that night, the lights inside each and every one of the towering casinos, as well as on the perpetually neon-studded strip, were dimmed for an entire minute in honor of The Voice. In the sudden deep blackout, just one marquee remained lit, featuring Frank's face. Maxine and I hadn't figured on that. Nice touch.

When the lights came back on, my mom looked out of our hotel room window at the marquee in front of the Mirage, and read aloud: "Francis—there are not enough towels in the world to dry our tears."

"It's true," she muttered, drying her own tears with a Mirage-logo'd cocktail napkin from the minibar.

I excused myself and went into the bathroom, where I couldn't help but weep. And not for Sinatra, but for my mom. For her struggles, the life she lived with my dad, and the life she lived now without him. My tears were primal, as reflexive a gesture as taking my mom's arm when we crossed the street or carrying her luggage even if together with mine it was too heavy to bear. I wanted to protect her, to shield her from pain, stave off disappointment.

That night, in a faux-marbled, fluorescent-lit hotel bathroom, I realized I had become the parent.

1999. The next year, several months before our scheduled trip, I started trying to talk Mom out of going to Vegas. "If we go, there's no telling who else will croak just to keep up our family tradition."

She didn't budge. I tried again.

"I made a list of beloved celebrities in failing health. Do you want the blood of Joe DiMaggio on your hands?"

But as much as I had been dreading the trip, Mom had been looking forward to it. So faster than you can say "Nudes on Ice," it was back to Hell.

This time Maxine couldn't come with us because of work (lucky her) so I was forced to deal with the torture alone. A couple of days before departure, as I was sharing my dread, my filmmaker friend Jane came up with a brilliant suggestion. "Why don't you take pictures and make a documentary of the trip?"

I lit up. A creative project was all I needed to shift my outlook.

And so, on our first day there, while Mom gambled to her heart's content, I busily set about taking pictures.

I posed my mother in insane tableaus . . .

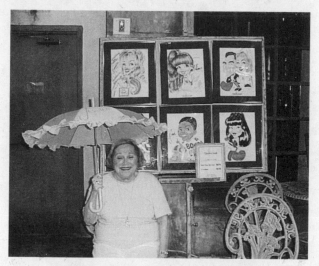

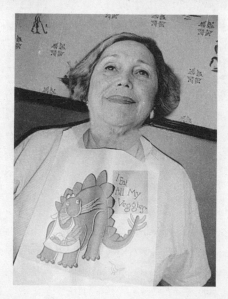

. . . and documented her winnings:

On the second morning in Vegas, we hit the Venetian early and found ourselves gambling at a row of slot machines with a gang of men and women who all towered over six feet. I caught a glimpse of the badge one of them was wearing. Of course. They were attending the Tip Toppers Tall Club convention.

By 11:30 we had worked up an appetite. We sat down for a meal at one of the hotel's restaurants, Delmonico's. At the table next to us sat a guy wearing a T-shirt that said, "I used to be schizophrenic, but now we're just fine." He was talking to his girlfriend in a too-loudy, Vegas-y voice, "I read that just last month Robin Leach was in that glass-walled 'private' room over there, and had six women take off all their clothes and cover themselves in whipped cream."

"Wait, they did that for the fat, old host from *Lifestyles of the Rich and Famous?*" his girlfriend gasped.

"Totally."

"Ewww. Gross."

The thought of that ancient Leach-lech egging on six whipped cream-swathed babes in public was enough to make me push away my Louisiana Lump Crab Cakes.

Then I saw it. Something familiar. A crowd gathering around one of the television sets at the bar. And I felt it, too. The buzz, the energy. The only thing that made hardened gamblers in Vegas stop for even a moment—*breaking news.*

I threw down my napkin and ran up to the TV. But wait, there was no death montage. Instead, on the screen, was just an image of the ocean. For a long time. Miles and miles of the sea and nothing else. "What is it? What's going on?" I asked the woman beside me. But before she could answer, I saw the crawl creeping along the bottom of the screen.

John F. Kennedy Jr.'s plane missing at sea.

I rushed back to our table. "Mom, I'm freaked," I said. "You're not gonna believe this." I told her the news.

"Oh my God," she blurted. "Didn't you meet JFK Jr. at Daryl Hannah's birthday party?"

"Yeah, we all ice skated together."

"Oh my God," she repeated, tears beginning to fill her eyes.

"Maybe they'll find him," I said, always optimistic.

"I hope to God they do," she whispered.

Apparently the gossiping gourmets at the table next to us hadn't heard the news or noticed the crowd at the bar. The guy continued his story. "The girls started licking the whipped cream off each other, then Robin Leach poured chocolate on one of their asses! He probably licked it clean!"

Hellooo! John F. Kennedy Jr.'s plane is missing at sea, motherfuckers!

"Mom, can we get out of here?"

"Absolutely," she said. "Let's go back to the room."

As we each sat on our separate double beds and watched the television coverage, I couldn't help but document the moment.

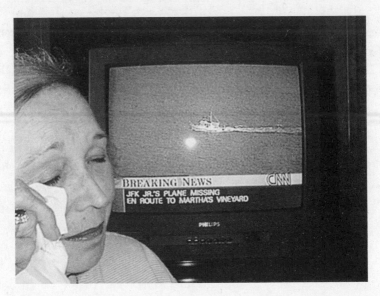

"That family has had nothing but tragedies," Mom said, her voice thick with tears.

"Yeah."

"It makes you really count your blessings, doesn't it?"

Boy did it ever. I was so grateful for them all. Especially for my mom. For all she'd ever done for me, for all she'd ever been for me. She was alive and well and doing the best she could.

I decided right then and there that, damn it, I was going to forever put aside my own personal Hell so I could help my mother feel Heaven on Earth.

"So Mom," I asked, "who do you think will kick the bucket when we come back next year?"

I climbed over to the other bed and sat close to her. "Let's place bets," I said. "Double or nothing. Liza Minnelli."

My mom perked up. "I'll take some of that action. My money's on Ronald Reagan." She laughed. The sparkle was back. Jackpot.

2004

❋ The house in L.A. that I sold because I no longer felt inspired there is where the new owner, Alexander Payne, creates one of this year's most lauded films, *Sideways*. (And even names a character after my housemate, Ken Cortland!)

❋ When President Bush calls for a constitutional amendment banning gay marriage, despite our "fear of commitment," Maxine and I make an appointment in San Francisco to get married as an act of civil disobedience. The California Supreme Court orders a halt to gay marriages two days before our wedding date.

❋ The CIA admits that there was no imminent threat from weapons of mass destruction before the U.S. invasion of Iraq. Thousands of troops and civilians have been killed in the war that Bush declared was over in 2003.

❋ *Friends* ends after a ten-year run, *Frasier* after eleven years, and *Sex and the City* after six. Meanwhile, to help my mother retire, I sell our family business for her, closing the doors after a sixty-year run.

❋ Two blows at the Jews—Mel Gibson's *The Passion of the Christ* and sacred kabbalah bracelets for sale at Target.

✳ I volunteer for presidential candidate Senator John Kerry, calling thousands of Democrats in Ohio and urging them to vote. We'll never know if their votes were really even counted or not.

✳ While I start planning a comeback of Angel and the Reruns, my "all-girl, all ex-con band," Martha Stewart goes to jail to serve a five-month sentence.

✳ Trendy Uggs seem more of a wardrobe malfunction than does Janet Jackson's exposure of her right breast during the Super Bowl halftime show.

Finding the OH! in Oprah

I didn't always want to bitch-slap Oprah. In fact, I used to be impressed by her generosity, determination, entrepreneurial skills, and compassion over Wynonna's weight. But ever since I appeared on her show, it's been a different story.

It's nine years after that appearance, and Maxine and I are on a long-overdue vacation when she turns on the TV and says three words I never imagined she'd utter. "Let's watch *Oprah*."

I am stunned. "Are you on crack?" She knows that whenever I see or even hear mention of Oprah, my self-esteem plunges in Pavlovian response.

Maxine shrugs. "It's just that she's talking about her favorite restaurants today, and the local paper said one of them is here in Montecito."

We are renting a little house on the beach in a town we loved long before Oprah put it on the map with the purchase of her 55-million-dollar home, where she has sleepovers with her best friend, Gayle. And it's so incongruous seeing my hardworking girlfriend wanting—and actually having the time—to watch TV during the day, there is no way I can deny her.

"Go ahead," I say. "I'll just read."

Let's face it. The biggest thing that can happen to an author is to appear on *Oprah*. In 1995, when my book *Girl Power: Young Women Speak*

Out was released, I pulled out all the big guns in my effort to manifest this goal. I set my intention, chanted, affirmed, visualized, prayed, and, well, spent way more money on a publicist than I could afford or had earned from the book's advance. But I was determined.

While the publicist worked her expensive magic, Maxine and I took another long-overdue vacation. We went to New Orleans, a place neither of us had been. Despite the city's allure, I called home almost hourly to check my messages, as this was back in the days before cell phones. Our itinerary went something like: folk art stores, pay phone; jazz on Bourbon Street, pay phone; jambalaya, crawfish pie, chili gumbo, pay phone.

Then, on our third day, at some random phone booth in the French Quarter, I checked my messages, and there it was—like some New Orleans lucky gris-gris bag full of magical charms and amulets—a message from the publicist.

"We did it. You're going to be on *Oprah*."

Nothing could top the exhilaration I felt—not even the city's famous chicory coffee and beignets, which one day earlier had ranked high on my list. It was only when I beeped in and listened to the message for the third time that I actually heard the details: "They're dedicating the whole episode to you and your book."

I broke out into a sweat and had to sit down, neither of which was included in my previous visualizations.

I was so thrilled that I was going to appear on *Oprah* that I didn't mind a bit when, three weeks later, the episode's producer called and asked for some pre-production help. Since my book included writings from teenage girls from all walks of life, the producer had decided she wanted six girls from the book to appear on *Oprah* with me; she also wanted to pepper throughout the show pre-taped segments of twenty additional girls reading their excerpts from the book. So one year after writing *Girl Power*, I had to track down the twenty-six girls she'd selected, no small feat since most had moved or gone off to college. This could have been quite enjoyable sleuthing work for me—*had there been a little thing called Google at the time*. As it was, I had to make an average of five calls per girl to finally locate them all (that's 130 calls total, but who's counting?).

I talked to all the girls, and from my conversations narrowed the list to six for the producer's approval. When some didn't work out, I had to pick others, then still others, until, at last, the final six were set.

Oh, but my job wasn't finished. I then had to obtain permission and signed releases from the girls' parents and legal guardians, get copies of the books to all of the girls so they'd know what writing of theirs they would be reading, and sift through thousands of submissions I had received so I could find, gather, and then FedEx each of the twenty-six pieces in the girls' original handwriting. All in two weeks. But I was more than happy to do everything the producer asked. After all, I was going to appear on *Oprah*.

June 5, 1995

Maxine and my ex (and still good friend) Danielle fly with me to Chicago on Oprah's Official Carrier—American Airlines, Something Special in the Air. I have so often heard the announcer at the end of each show tell us that "Guests of the *Oprah Winfrey Show* stay at the All-Suites Omni Hotel, located in the heart of Chicago's Magnificent Mile," and I still can't quite believe that one of those "guests" is now me.

After we check into our room, which, according to the plaque on the door is the Authors Suite (and let me tell you, I'm feelin' like an author—I'm going to appear on *Oprah*!), we find three of the six girls who have arrived, and we all go out to dinner. The teens are bubbling with confidence, totally psyched for tomorrow's taping. I play along like I am, too, but actually, I'm scared shitless. I haven't performed in years, and I've been much happier behind the scenes. And even when I was performing, I always managed to hide behind either a character (like Angel) or something distracting (like juggling and fire-eating).

This is the first time since Art Linkletter's *House Party* that I am going to have to appear on television as just *me*.

The next morning my fear intensifies when I wake with a start from a nightmare in which I was on Oprah's stage in front of a huge studio audience, completely naked, except for two large cinnamon buns I held in front of my breasts.

I take a long hot shower and pull myself together. The limo picks us up and we're whisked to Harpo Studios, where a production assistant leads me to the green room. I take deep breaths to calm down, and I almost succeed—until I see the breakfast spread, which includes large cinnamon buns. I don't let my breasts anywhere near them.

I am greeted by the producer, whom I've chatted with day and night for the past two weeks, and we hug like we're old friends. As she ushers me into the makeup room, she informs me that this is the last day of taping before Oprah's hiatus. *Great.* I'm sure Oprah's mind is already in Hawaii, sitting at a luau eating four-ounce protein portions of roast pig and baked-not-fried taro chips. I try to talk myself down, but it's not helping that the makeup woman is shaping my eyebrows into severe Cruella De Vil arches.

O's a professional, I silently tell myself. Even though it's her last show of the season, she'll be focused. No doubt she read the book—or at least skimmed it. She'll relate to the adolescent tales of hardship; she'll weep, clutch the book to her bosom, and proclaim: "I LOVE *GIRL POWER*. EVERYONE SHOULD READ THIS BOOK," catapulting it to the bestseller list. I have faith in Oprah.

The producer takes me and my scary eyebrows into the hallway to meet up with the girls. Then she escorts all seven of us onto the stage. The studio audience has already been seated. My heart races when I see the familiar *Oprah* set, where just this morning I sat naked, and it slows only a bit when I find Maxine and Danielle in the audience, radiating strength and comfort. The producer seats each of the teen girls on the stage until, like some tragic musical chairs game, I am left standing. I laugh off the mistake until the producer takes me by the arm.

"Come with me," she says.

She then leads me to my seat . . . IN THE AUDIENCE.

I am thrown into a rinse cycle of emotions. *I'm baffled*—had they told me I wouldn't be on the stage but I missed that tiny detail in the pre-prod prep frenzy, or just blocked it out altogether? *I'm furious*—I'm not up there, representing MY book. *I'm relieved*—I won't be so nervous if all eyes aren't on me. *I'm ashamed*—this should be all about the girls anyway, not me. But mostly I feel ripped-off. How will viewers think the girls got here? That Oprah just happened upon them? Her producers searched high and low for them? Damn it, I spent almost two years crisscrossing the country, leading writing workshops for teen mothers and girls in gangs, participating at powwows and rodeos, attending surfing competitions on far-flung beaches and open mic nights at inner-city hip-hop joints, judging a teen beauty contest, and volunteering at a residential treatment center for at-risk girls. I nurtured, encouraged, and collected these girls' writings, and then I included their excerpts with my own writing so that I could help give them, and other teen girls, a forum, a voice, an opportunity to speak out. These are *my* girls, damn it, they're not Oprah's. My hands are shaking.

As the show begins, I look around the audience and find my editor, who has flown in from New York. She gives me a "Don't worry, it's okay" nod. I stare straight ahead so I don't risk catching a glimpse of Maxine and Danielle—I know they're just as upset for me as I am, and I'm already on the brink of tears.

Oprah waltzes onstage and the audience goes wild. She shares about her early years of abuse, and feeling like she didn't belong. Right on. Then she introduces the girls and casually mentions that they have "participated in a new book." An image of the cover flashes on the monitors. Okay, this might be okay. At least the book will get some publicity.

But soon it begins to feel like pre-hiatus O hasn't read my book, hasn't skimmed it or even read the *description* on the back cover. She says everything she's supposed to say, reading off the cue cards, and throws in little anecdotes about her own adolescence that seem to be ad-libbed, but when pictures of her, correlating to each tale, flash on the video screen behind her, I see they're *so* not.

When one of the girls reads her excerpt FROM MY BOOK, Oprah beams and nods—she can relate. When another girl reads her piece FROM MY BOOK, and her eyes well up with tears, Oprah starts to weep. But she makes little connection, and little mention, that these pieces are FROM MY BOOK. There is no clutching it to her bosom, no "EVERYONE SHOULD READ THIS BOOK." There's not even a copy of the book anywhere in sight. And I'm still sitting in the audience watching the six girls, as well as the twenty others who, at every commercial break and every time the show returns after the commercial, appear in the video montages, their voice-overs reading excerpts FROM MY BOOK.

At one point Oprah leads into a break by saying, "How do TV commercials and magazine ads featuring ultra-thin super models make teen girls feel? We're gonna ask our girls in just a moment."

Our girls??? YO, O, *my* girls!

Despite feeling completely dissed, I must confess the episode does move me. The girls onstage are confident, smart, and eloquent. I beam like a proud mother to them all. When they read, I feel the same chills I did when I first discovered those voices. I weep and cheer for the girls. Still, as Oprah continues to talk about everything EXCEPT the book, I sneak glances at my watch. Fifteen minutes have passed and I've not said a word; she hasn't even introduced me. A half hour goes by. Then forty-five minutes. I've clawed trenches in my palms.

And then, finally, fifty minutes in, Oprah introduces me. I hear my heart pounding in my ears—*hold it together*, I chant silently. Oprah first asks me to share my favorite quote from a girl, one that I opened *Girl Power* with. I gladly do: "Sometimes paper is the only thing that will listen to you." A bit prophetic as when I try to say a bit more, Oprah doesn't listen to me—she interrupts me. She says how *she* always encourages teen girls to write and keep journals. She asks me a few more questions, inserts her own thoughts on the topic, and suddenly my two minutes are up. That's it. I am stunned.

Soon the show is over, and as the audience files out, the producer motions me up to the stage. Maybe she wants to apologize? Finally acknowledge that *Girl Power* is my book, and the great show she got out of the girls was because they were from my book?

I hurry toward her. But no apology. Apparently it's customary that still photographs be taken of each of the show's guests with Oprah. At least she remembers I am a guest. First the photographer snaps a picture of Oprah with the girls and me, then one of each of us alone with O. I raise my pencil-arched eyebrows and smile, doing everything I can to disguise my disappointment. Then we're escorted out, and we each receive a memento—a white ceramic coffee mug signed with "*Thanks*, Oprah" in teal glaze.

I spend years finding these girls and writing my book, hire an expensive publicist to get me on *Oprah*, work my ass off for the episode's producer, sit in the studio audience being virtually ignored by O, and all I got was this lousy "*Thanks*, Oprah" mug?!

That night, back in the All-Suites Omni Hotel located in the heart of Chicago's Magnificent Mile, my supportive girlfriend and friend try to convince me that no matter what, the exposure will be great for the book. If it doesn't catapult it to the bestseller list, it will at least have a huge impact on sales. After all, they flashed the cover, and they did show the pages of the book with the pieces the girls read in the montages on the video screen. Those typed words had to come from *somewhere*; surely viewers will make the connection and run out and buy the book. After the episode airs, I will crack open the Sunday *Times* and see *Girl Power* on the bestseller list right alongside *Dave Barry's Complete Guide to Guys*. Yeah. Sure.

Three months later the show finally airs, and although they've put together an inspiring episode—which does make me happy—watching it forces me to replay that day. Of course I am on for only two minutes, talking from the audience, and there is little mention of the book. The show doesn't affect sales in the least. How could an author's book featured on *Oprah* for an entire episode not see a sales spike? Just ask me (and Carnie Wilson).

In Montecito, while Maxine watches *Oprah,* as much as I try to read, I'm drawn in. Damn that Oprah! How dare she grab my attention? For the past nine years, ever since I SORT OF appeared on her show, I've felt dejected and rejected whenever I've seen or heard anything about Oprah. And I've been pissed. Not enough to throw my *"Thanks,* Oprah" gift mug to the floor and shatter it, but definitely enough to relegate it to a closet where no beverage would ever remind me of the day I was slighted by Oprah.

Even though I logically know Oprah had nothing to do with what happened on my episode, and that her producers put it together, ever since then, I've always found fault with Oprah. Sure she gave away cars, but she didn't pony up a penny for them—it was all an ad ploy for General Motors—and on top of that, all the "people in need" were forced to pay taxes on the cars. And on that very same infamous car giveaway episode, I'm told she fulfilled a deprived girl's dream by giving her a hug and a college scholarship. But was the beauty makeover necessary?

Every day near my house I pass a billboard announcing each new *Oprah* episode, and I laugh at the inane topic titles: "Solve my Decorating Dilemma," "Depressed, Mentally Ill, and Famous," "Oprah Cleans Out Her Closet." (Guess who was in the closet with her? Her best friend, Gayle!)

Basically, for the last nine years I've wanted to bitch-slap Oprah.

But there in our rented beach house, as I try to ignore the show, I can't help but feel moved by the story of how Oprah saved a woman's failing Sandwich Shoppe by giving her the money to carry on.

Hillary Carlip

"See?" Maxine remarks. "You can't deny all the good she does. She helps tons of people throughout the world with her Angel Network, and now, after eating a delicious curried chicken sandwich with shredded carrots on spicy white pepper-jack, she gave this woman the dough to carry on. No pun intended."

"I know, I know," I say. "She's a saint. But why should I give her my respect when she showed me so little?"

As hard as I try to let my disappointment go, watching Oprah—even nine years later—makes me feel like shit all over again. Like I blew it. Like I'm somehow not enough.

Then a strange thing happens. Sitting there listening to the waves crashing against the front deck, I begin to see that the feeling of not being enough has always been at the core of my life. That's why when I was eight I pretended to be other people, why I befriended stars when I was fourteen and started juggling and eating fire at fifteen. That's why in my twenties I hid behind invented characters, and why in my thirties I dated gorgeous actresses and models. I've been working on this issue all my life, and here I am in my forties, still struggling with sagging self-esteem.

And then all of a sudden it's like Oprah hears my thoughts rattling and wants to make it all up to me. Make amends for her behavior of almost a decade ago. Give me something the way she gives to so many others. I can't believe what I see.

She's sitting onstage with her guest, Dr. Maya Angelou, who is there to talk about her new cookbook. Oprah declares, "I'm so proud of this book because in the dedication Maya says. . . . " She opens it and reads: "I dedicate this book to every wannabe cook who will dare criticism by getting into the kitchen and stirring up some groceries. And—*LISTEN!* . . . "

Oprah says the word "listen" like she's a child about to tell her parents about her first day at school. "To O, who said she wanted a big, pretty cookbook. Well, Honey, here you are."

"*I LOVE IT!!*" Oprah squeals.

Suddenly she seems so tiny. So vulnerable. There's the inimitable Oprah Winfrey overjoyed by this validation, by Maya Angelou's recognition of her. After all she has accomplished, after all the adulation she's received, even Oprah still doesn't feel like she's enough.

In that moment I stop wanting to bitch-slap Oprah. Instead, I want to take the precious, unacknowledged girl in my arms. I want to comfort her, applaud her, even provide her with a makeover.

There in our rented beach house, sitting with the love of my life—my partner of twelve years—I finally get it. I may *never* feel like I'm enough. But suddenly, that's okay. It's what has propelled me into countless escapades, forced me to continually create and express, fueled me with the mission to inspire and make a difference, and caused me to welcome limitless possibilities by doing everything unaccording to plan. And if not feeling like I'm enough can do for me anything close to what it's done for Oprah, hell, I have no complaints.

So the next time I appear on *Oprah*, sitting next to her ON THE STAGE, I'll bring along my mug and raise it in a toast to her. After all, "*Thanks*, Oprah" has taken on new meaning.

Hillary Carlip

HILLARY CARLIP
"GIRL POWER"

HARPO
T.O.W.S.
HILLARY CARLIP
GR/2   6/6

Thanks!

Thanks!
-O-
GIRL POWER!

Acknowledgments

BIG, PHAT SHOUT-OUTS TO:

God, Goddess, Mastermind, Higher Power—all the forces at my spiritual buffet—for countless and infinite blessings.

Mim and Bob (wherever you are, Dad!), for all your support, encouragement and love. You're the best parents a girl could ever have. And Howard, Bro, YOU ROCK!

Sister-wives Michelle Boyaner (my creative partner in crime) and Barbara Green, for too many things to enumerate.

Amy Friedman, for your input, feedback, skilled eye, brilliant notes, and love of the personal essay. You inspire so many of us.

Mim Eichler, for your incredible insights and huge contributions.

Katie Ford, Nancy Fichman, and "Chance," for always working your magic.

Laurie Liss, agent and friend extraordinaire, for your spectacular ideas (the front pieces in particular!) and your faith in me, and my work.

Alison Callahan—my awesome, tireless editor, for constant support and enthusiasm, and the rest of the kick-ass team at Harper Paperbacks—Carrie Kania, Hope Innelli, David Roth-Ey, Jennifer Hart, Jeanette Perez, Beth Silfin, Shannon Valcich, Casey Kait, May Vlachos, Virginia Stanley, Brian McSharry, Kathy Smith, Jeanette Zwart, Carla Clifford, David Youngstrom, Mark Hillesheim, Leslie Cohen, Keonaona Peterson, and Kolt Beringer.

Mary Schuck, Elliott Beard, Robin Bilardello, and anyone else in the art department at HarperCollins who worked on this—for your patience, and for being so open to my input.

Jenny Hart, amazing artist and stitcher, for helping make my vision real.

So many of my peeps who have been along for the ride, generously offering input, ideas, support, and friendship—Jill Soloway, Danielle Eskinazi, Wendy Melvoin, Lisa Cholodenko, Jane Anderson, Tess Ayers, Dewey Reid, Cindy Reid, Kristin Hahn, Charlie Stringer, Sally Lapiduss, Lynnie Greene, Sharon Morrill, Miriam Cutler, Michele Kort, Deborah and Diane Gibson, Caryn Karmatz-Rudy, Laurie Notaro, Elaine Pope, Marcus Charalambous and the rest of the dudes at Backbone, Jane Ford, Crescent Orpelli, Esther and Saul Lapiduss, and Gregory Poe.

My Bday Think Tank and pals, for brill PR ideas and general lovin'—Allee Willis, Prudence Fenton, Paul Reubens, Tania Katan, Angela Ellsworth, Susie Mosher, Hope Royaltey, Adele House, Jennifer Hoppe, Jackie Marchand, Kathleen Beaton, Rogers Hartmann, Mimi Friedman, Carolyn Strauss, Candy Trabuco, Lisa Coleman, Renata Kanclerz, Ken Cortland, Alan Marx, Sam Christensen, Marshall Johnson, Wendy Miller, Carmen Carrasco, Erika Schroeder, Bob Garrett,

Stan Zimmerman, Julia Salazar, James Nocito, Al Harp, Carole Murray, and Leni Schwendinger.

My fellow writers in Amy's East Side Posse, and the original West Side group, for your input and support—Lauren Tom, Alan Olifson, Michelle Boyaner, Shannon Morris, Karman Kregloe, Denise Gill, Holly Tarson, Yvonne Chotzen, Cheryl Montelle, Maggie Walker, Andrew Harmon, Isabel Story, Robyn Travis, Anita Phillips, and especially Gali Kronenberg for sharp insight and skilled editing early on.

All past, present, and future contributors to FRESH YARN. It has been a pleasure and honor working with you all.

My L.A. peeps, who have created spoken word events that I've thoroughly enjoyed performing, and honing my pieces, at. Maggie Rowe and Jill Soloway (Sit 'n' Spin); Meredith Scott Lynn and Cynthia Moore (Word-A-Rama); Beth Lapides and Greg Miller (Un-Cabaret's Say the Word), Annabelle Gurwitch (Fired!) and so many others in L.A. and throughout the country—thanks for creating a place for so many to be inspired.

Nanielle Devereaux, my sistah and dear friend. I miss you so much even though you're always with me. And thanks to the tribe, who carries her spirit on in the world.

My boys, Homey and Slim. All love. All the time.

And what can I say to Maxine Lapiduss? My oddball soul mate, the everything girl. Thanks for reading endless drafts, giving genius notes, being patient when I'd be up at 4:00 a.m. working, your constant love and inspiration, and for being the one to encourage me to tell my stories in the first place.